DISCO IS
STAR WARS, FANTASIA,
THE FOURTH OF JULY,
AND *CLOSE ENCOUNTERS*
OF THE WILDEST KIND!

Now you can experience *Saturday Night Fever* any night or day of the week with one book that takes you into all the discos around, from such elites as New York New York to small-town hustle palaces and entertainment emporiums. You'll meet all the regulars from well-known celebrities to Roller-Arena, who's never been seen with his skates off, and that quiet guy who always shows up with the same date—a life-size, blow-up female doll! You'll discover how to mix and match all those chic and zany disco fashions, and find out how to rent your own private deejay or start your own disco. You'll learn all the latest steps and the best kinds of props to have on hand. And you'll be able to hustle your way right on to the disco scene. All it takes is a quick look through

Big Bestsellers from SIGNET

- ☐ **SONG OF SOLOMON by Toni Morrison.** (#E8340—$2.50)*
- ☐ **GIFTS OF LOVE by Charlotte Vale Allen.** (#J8388—$1.95)*
- ☐ **BELLADONNA by Erica Lindley.** (#J8387—$1.95)*
- ☐ **THE BRACKENROYD INHERITANCE by Erica Lindley.** (#W6795—$1.50)
- ☐ **THE DEVIL IN CRYSTAL by Erica Lindley.** (#E7643—$1.75)
- ☐ **PRESIDENTIAL EMERGENCY by Walter Stovall.** (#E8371—$2.25)*
- ☐ **THE GODFATHER by Mario Puzo.** (#E8508—$2.50)*
- ☐ **KRAMER VERSUS KRAMER by Avery Corman.** (#E8282—$2.50)
- ☐ **VISION OF THE EAGLE by Kay McDonald.** (#J8284—$1.95)*
- ☐ **CRESSIDA by Clare Darcy.** (#E8287—$1.75)*
- ☐ **DANIEL MARTIN by John Fowles.** (#E8249—$2.95)
- ☐ **THE EBONY TOWER by John Fowles.** (#E8254—$2.50)
- ☐ **THE FRENCH LIEUTENANT'S WOMAN by John Fowles.** (#E8535—$2.50)
- ☐ **RIDE THE BLUE RIBAND by Rosalind Laker.** (#J8252—$1.95)*
- ☐ **THE SILVER FALCON by Evelyn Anthony.** (#E8211—$2.25)

*Price slightly higher in Canada

If you wish to order these titles,
please see the coupon in
the back of this book.

PHOTO AND LIGHTING BY DESIGN CIRCUIT, INC.

DISCO FEVER

by Kitty Hanson

A SIGNET BOOK
NEW AMERICAN LIBRARY
TIMES MIRROR

NAL BOOKS ARE ALSO AVAILABLE AT DISCOUNTS IN BULK
QUANTITY FOR INDUSTRIAL OR SALES-PROMOTIONAL USE.
FOR DETAILS, WRITE TO PREMIUM MARKETING DIVISION,
NEW AMERICAN LIBRARY, INC., 1301 AVENUE OF THE
AMERICAS, NEW YORK, NEW YORK 10019.

Copyright © 1978 by Kitty Hanson

All rights reserved.

SIGNET TRADEMARK REG. U.S. PAT. OFF. AND FOREIGN COUNTRIES
REGISTERED TRADEMARK—MARCA REGISTRADA
HECHO EN CHICAGO, U.S.A.

SIGNET, SIGNET CLASSICS, MENTOR, PLUME AND MERIDIAN BOOKS
are published by The New American Library, Inc.,
1301 Avenue of the Americas, New York, New York 10019

First Signet Printing, November, 1978

1 2 3 4 5 6 7 8 9

PRINTED IN THE UNITED STATES OF AMERICA

For Hal,
who started this disco adventure
in the first place,
for
his patience, his support,
his encouragement, and
his fantastic form on the disco floor

Acknowledgments

The thank-yous and acknowledgments that usually precede a book are, for the writer, really the most fun to write. For one thing, it means that you've finished the book. For another, it provides an opportunity to remember and re-experience all of the chance, choice, and charming (and some not-so-charming) encounters that have contributed to the work that finally winds up between the covers.

A book like this one, in particular, requires the goodwill and cooperation of a wide, and sometimes wild, variety of people, for the disco phenomenon is one that cuts a broad swath across our society. What other single subject could have offered a writer the opportunity of picking the brains of authorities in music, theater, fashion, electronics, dance, medicine, economics, engineering, history, sociology, psychiatry?

Some of the people who made it possible to put this book together were simply performing their jobs in a purely professional capacity, but deserve our thanks because they said "yes" when they could just as easily have said "no."

And then there are those who not only said "yes," but who volunteered their time, their talent, which one could never buy—and certainly not hope to repay.

William Pitt, III

If it were true, as Truman Capote has claimed, that there are only 500 people who make New York happen, William Pitt, III, would have to be one of them, for he is deeply and actively involved in New York society's philanthropic activities and nightlife. A dedicated discophile, he has been our enthusiastic counselor, door opener, and guide into the wonderful world of disco.

Very early in the development of the current disco phenomenon, Bill became familiar with the exciting discotheques of the world through his work with Prince Alexis Obolensky in promoting the first Backgammon Tournaments that made the game so popular in this country. He organized tournaments in Athens, Monte Carlo, Las Vegas, and other cities at home, abroad, and in the Caribbean, and seldom missed a disco in the process. Backgammon is one of the most popular "pluses" at the country's most plush and exclusive discotheques today.

For a time, Bill managed Great Scott, considered the most elegant discotheque in the Hamptons, on Long Island, and his expertise as a disco consultant grows out of his experience on both sides of the disco floor—as a dancer and as a club manager. Now that he is living in the Big Apple, his name is frequent and familiar in society news as the organizer and spark plug of prestigious charity balls and benefits. He is consultant to the disco New York New York.

Bill, who grew up commuting between Southampton, Palm Beach, and Greenwich, Connecticut, recently developed an analysis of the art of social climbing which he calls the "Palm Beach game." Many of the elements of that game are inherent—and apparent—in the games that people play at discotheques, particularly in the phenomenon of "the door game" in the so-called trendy clubs.

In the relatively new social arena of the discotheque, Bill Pitt is probably one of the most generally knowledgeable people around. And one of the nicest.

Discothekin' Magazine

Three young, native New Yorkers with an idea and an incredible store of determination, optimism, and know-how are the brains (and often the brawn) behind *Discothekin'* Magazine, which may be on its way to becoming *the* trade-consumer publication in the disco field.

Discothekin' has had a bumpy off-again-on-again career since Alex Kabbaz conceived the idea in 1975, and started publication in 1976 with the editorial help and assistance of Nicole Semhon, and with Al Zucaro's $1,000, which, says Alex, "was all we thought it would take to produce a nationally distributed consumer magazine"!

Kabbaz, who in 1974 had worked as a nighttime disco deejay and a daytime apprentice to the unsuccessful *Harper's Weekly*, decided to use his two talents to put out his own disco publication. He copyrighted the magazine in 1975. Nicole, an NYU student and patron of the disco where Alex had worked, succeeded him as the deejay and then later deserted the turntables for the typewriter at *Discothekin'*. Zucaro, a restaurateur and disco-operator for whom Alex had once worked, completed the troika in March, 1976.

By September, 1976, *Discothekin'* had a staff of twenty-two and a severe case of overextension. It almost went out of business. With the financial help of all three sets of parents, the three started over again, and finally arrived at *Discothekin' "B,"* a trade publication supported by advertising and subscriptions.

Although it is small and not yet in the circulation (or income) class of some of the older publications around, *Discothekin'* today finds itself increasingly regarded as the real "horse's mouth" of the disco field. It deserves the reputation. What Alex Kabbaz, Al Zucaro, and Nicole Semhon do not know about disco is not worth bothering about, and their generosity with their files, photos, and experience has been invaluable.

And. . . . but not least

Rita Hamilton, fashion editor of the *Daily News Record*
Robert Melendez, fashion illustrator for *Women's Wear Daily*
John Monte, National Dance Director, and Charles Casanave, president, Fred Astaire National Dance Association, Inc.
James Bourne and Sherry Peregrin
Benita Garfinkel of the *Hollywood Reporter*
Nancy Karen
Louis Nemeth
Darleen Rubin
Gerard Barnier
Wide World Photos

New York *Daily News*
Tim Boxer
Kleb Associates
Marlene Backer and Stewart Feinstein, Le Clique
Larry Silverman and Billboard Publications, Inc.
Robert Lobi, president, Design Circuit, Inc.
Howard Rheiner, Lite Lab
Don de Natale
Andrea Baruffi and Adam Tihany
Harvey Kirk
Michael Bux

and

all of my journalist colleagues across the country who provided a picture of the national disco scene

as well as

Atlantic Records, Casablanca Records/and Film Works, Robert Stigwood Organization, Island Records, Polydor Records, TK Records, Curtom Records, Private Stock Records, Butterfly Records, London Records, Warner Brothers Records, RCA Records,

and most important

my mother, who didn't get a phone call for weeks!

Contents

Acknowledgments ix
1. Disco Inferno 1
2. We Came to Play 10
3. The Grand Tour 16
4. If My Friends Could See Me Now 35
5. Stayin' Alive 56
6. Risky Changes 68
7. You've Got Magic 81
8. Let's All Chant 117
9. The Beat Goes On 136
10. Night Fever 158
11. Once Upon a Time 173
12. At the Discotheque 178
13. I Think I'm Gonna Fall 193
14. Dance with Me 198
15. Last Dance 234

PHOTO AND LIGHTING BY DESIGN CIRCUIT, INC.

DISCO FEVER

Disco Inferno

Long before you hear it, you can feel it—a throbbing beat that pulses in the floor and in the air. Then you hear that unmistakable disco sound, pushed through a forest of speakers and hurled against the eardrums at a volume close to pain. Light shapes swim out of the dark; they flash and spiral dizzily, and endlessly repeat themselves in the mirrored walls. Revolving wheels of tinted lights splash the room with color, and a thousand facets of spinning mirrored globes fracture the light beams and engulf the dancers in swirling galaxies of stars.

Then, at the feet of the dancers, a scented mist begins to rise, and soon the pounding boots, the stiletto heels and platform soles are hidden. Slowly, the weaving bodies and swaying arms fade into a swirling fog, and the room is filled with dancing demons. . . .

This is the world of disco.

It's "Star Wars," it's "Fantasia!" it's the Fourth of July and "Close Encounters" of the wildest kind—all at once and in one place. It's a world of sexuality and sensuality, of escapism and play—an unreal, surreal world of sound and music, born out of the new and growing wave of dance fever.

Disco dancing, once the electronic night rite of a far-out few, has become a national mania, spawning a new kind of night life, changing the way that people dress and play and live, the way they spend their money—and the way they spend their time. After nearly a decade of letting music go to their heads instead of to their feet, Americans are dancing again.

Discomania is becoming the cultural phenomenon of the seventies.

People today are dancing more than at any time since the Great Depression, and discotheques are on their way to becoming to the seventies what dance halls were to the

Dancers swirl in a scented mist at New York New York
1978 DISCOTHEKIN' NEWS/DOCUMENT ARCHIVES

thirties. And the dance "maniacs" are not just the young and the famous, but people of all ages and occupations.

In the world of disco, bizarre costumes and exotic masquerade mingle with haute couture and celebrity chic to create a unique environment that is part showbiz, part Mardi Gras, part café society. Here is where celebrities come to be nobodies; and where nobodies come to be stars for a night. Here is where stars like Farrah and Liz and Bianca come to celebrate their birthdays . . . where Liza Minnelli unwinds after a strenuous night on stage . . . where Mikhail Baryshnikov dances after dancing . . . where world heavyweight champion Leon Spinks celebrated his victory over Muhammad Ali.

It was in a discotheque in Brooklyn that John Travolta became a star. And it is in discotheques like that one, all across the country, that young Americans are finding excitement and release and moments of stardom in their own "Saturday Night Fever."

For about eighteen months preceding the release of the movie, there had been outbreaks of dance mania in widely separated parts of the country. Travolta and *Saturday Night Fever* turned it into an epidemic.

Within the past ten or twelve months, discomania has erupted like a volcano out of the underground clubs of New York and the West Coast, out of the ethnic neighborhoods, and the chic and private clubs of the wealthy, and has found itself an international phenomenon—a technology, an industry.

Disco music throbs over the airwaves of radio stations dedicated to the heavy disco beat, increasingly on the popular music stations, and in the background music of television commercials and dramas. All across the country, entertainment complexes are multiplying like clones—and the core cell is the discotheque.

For the first time in many years, a life-style trend has started on the East Coast and is moving, joyfully and irresistibly west. The soul and heartbeat of disco are still in New York, but the spirit is spreading.

What makes normal, healthy, hard-working people turn their lives inside out and their days upside down, dislocating their budgets and upsetting their biorhythms for a strenuous diversion that doesn't get going until nearly midnight and sends them yawning into the day?

"They come to celebrate the good things and to forget the bad ones," says the operator of a discotheque that caters to the young working class. "For a couple of hours a week, they can let it all hang out and just move and let the music fill their heads and push out everything else. For a little while, they can get away from their lives."

"It's fun!" says a young dancer. "It makes me feel good."

"Disco is a fantasy world," says a self-styled disco queen whose leisure and social life are built around the discotheques. "I need fantasy in my life. That's what most people are looking for these days."

Discotheques are like dandelions—they can sprout in the most unlikely places. A disco can be a chic little supper club with a postage-stamp floor in an exclusive hotel—or a super-barn of a dance hall created out of an erstwhile factory. There are discos in renovated lofts and machine shops, in former taverns and converted theaters. There's a disco in an abandoned soap factory; another in a savings and loan office. In the cities, they show up in refurbished mansions and recycled restaurants. Outside the metropolitan areas, they pop up in Holiday Inns and shopping centers, in one-time airport hangars, abandoned supermarkets, rural roadhouses, and neighborhood bars.

The tie that binds them all together is the music and the atmosphere of sensual, safe stimulation. The flashing lights, the pulsating rhythms, the erotic and exotic motions, the spectacles and illusions—these are what makes disco the epitome of where it's at today.

Within what the technicians call these "environments" on any given Friday or Saturday night (and increasingly during the week), you'll find jet-setters and Beautiful People, shipping clerks and plain Janes, the rich and the barely-making-it, the just-of-age and the past-middle-age, the gays and the straights, the well known and the scarcely noted. All have one thing in common: a compelling desire to shed their inhibitions and their nine-to-five skins in a night-long celebration of nonstop music and perpetual motion.

Whatever your age, race, color, dance, or sexual preferences, there's a discotheque somewhere for you. There are discos for blacks, for whites, for Latins; for people who want to Hustle and for those who prefer free-styling; for blue

Joyous frenzy at Infinity, New York's first neon disco
NEW YORK DAILY NEWS PHOTO

collar workers, white collar workers, and very rich non-workers.

But the most popular and most famous are those discos that are democratic playgrounds where *everybody* comes out to play.

Singles bars, those dreary mating grounds of the sixties, are on their way out. Originally planned as places to overcome loneliness, the singles bars have become lonely places themselves and are scornfully referred to these days as "meat racks." Discos are flashier, and the search does not seem so desperate. And you do not have to be a Woody Allen wit playing conversational "can-you-top-this?" at a bar. At a discotheque, you can enjoy the scene, the music, and the dancing, and can bump into a potential friend in a natural and unpressured way. "I Fell in Love While Dancing" is not a popular disco tune for nothing.

But while the majority of disco dancers—perhaps about 70 percent—are under forty and probably single, more and more older and married people are succumbing to disco fever. It's a great exercise, they say. It's a stress-reliever, a fantasy trip, a social encounter. It can also be a lot of fun.

Sociologists, psychologists, and other people-watchers have a variety of explanations for the current epidemic of discomania. Some alarmists—like those who saw imminent decline in the hula hoop and the mini skirt—see it as the prelude to a new age of hedonism. A nation of self-indulgers, they say, will forsake their political and social responsibilities and devote their time and money to the pursuit of pleasure and sensation. The discotheques, they warn, will become pleasure palaces of decadent delights.

There are those who can hardly wait!

But other sociologists see the current dance mania as part of modern man's revolt against being a perpetual spectator.

Over the years, they say, the majority of us have done less and less participating and more and more watching, as the more talented and better trained among us express themselves in sports, music, drama, and dance. We watch football; we watch baseball; we watch movies and endless hours of television. We've been letting other people do all the singing and dancing and playing—and having all the fun. Now we're getting restless.

A nation of do-it-yourself machinists, home-builders, and fix-it people is getting itchy for some do-it-yourself entertainment.

Unlike the customers of nightclubs or cabarets who pay their money and then sit back to be entertained, the customers at discotheques are paying their money to entertain themselves. It's the people who are the real show at the discos—and they haven't come to be critical or to find fault. They've come to play.

"It's as though somebody's giving a party and you're invited," a twenty-three-year-old discophile said, summing up as well as any sociologist the spirit of today's disco dance madness.

It's party time in the USA, and everyone's been invited.

We Came to Play

"There's something that happens to you when you see all those people waiting outside the door. You sort of, well, pull yourself up, your adrenaline starts to pump with a kind of disco beat, and you sort of *march* right up there. I prefer to get out of the cab down the block a little bit, because there's the whole approach you must assume in order to just sort of—arrive. If your attitude is, 'I belong, therefore, here I am' then you get in. If you hesitate—or seem too eager, you're lost."

It is known as "the door game," and it is played, with variations, at every good or "in"—and certainly successful—discotheque in the country. The rules of the game are very simple: Some people get in; others stay out. The only thing that varies from disco to disco is "who."

"We try not to let potential problems in," says one successful operator, Jay Levey, who runs Infinity, one of the most exciting and popular discos in New York City. "A good disco owner makes sure that all his troubles are at the door. It's a lot smarter to keep the hitters out than to try to ride herd on them after they're in."

At Jubilation, Paul Anka's new $3-million disco in Las Vegas, guests enter through a metal detector, as in an airport, to make certain no guns or knives get in.

But there's more to the game than security. Whether it is a matter of letting celebrities in or just keeping troublemakers out, to the owner of a discotheque the door game is a matter of survival. The people who want in think that it's the music, the decor, the lighting that makes the disco environment. The owner knows it's the people.

It is people who make a discotheque and it is people who can break it. That is why so many discos are set up as clubs, charging dues or fees that range from $100 to $1,000 a year—

that than anyone will admit. And that is why we're all dying to get in. It always makes a place popular if it's hard to get into."

The psychological benefits of being chosen add up to financial profits for the choos*ers*—the discotheque owners—and many of them create a waiting line if they don't have one.

In suburbs or small towns where the wave of discomania is just beginning to break, discos still "have a bad name," says Julie, a young discophile in Mendota, Illinois, which is a little "too far" away from Chicago for weekly disco-ing.

"It's because, in order for them to make money, they have to let everybody in. And when you let just anybody in," she adds, "you have trouble."

Fights, shoving matches, and other unpleasantnesses do occur at some discos—especially at the seamier clubs where someone is cashing in on the current dance mania to turn a fast dollar and doesn't care much about what happens after that dollar is in the till.

But as *Saturday Night Fever* carries the dance virus across the country, the sophisticated decor, lighting, and sound of the cosmopolitan clubs will follow—and so will the sophisticated techniques of playing the door game.

While other discos around the country may not play the game as flamboyantly as it is played at Studio 54, at every successful disco it is a very serious game indeed. It is played at lush and lavish Zorine's in Chicago where the membership is tight and the dues are out of sight; and at Chicago's BBC, which is a public disco. It is played at Penrod's, the chic spot in Atlanta, at the new Scaramouche in Miami, at El Privado in Los Angeles where the membership fee is $1,000 a year—and at Dillon's, in L.A., a more-or-less public place. It is even played at the Rainforest in the Hilton Hotel in New Orleans where, technically speaking, there isn't even a door.

At all of the Regine's around the world, the door game is played through a hole in the door. In the New York Regine's a small glass panel slides aside to allow the Outs to be studied before they become Ins. At Hippopotamus, one of the most enduring discos in the country, having survived the first rise and fall of discotheques, guests are screened discreetly through a peephole that is scarcely noticeable.

At New York New York, a disco whose personality is urbane and Great Gatsby cool, the game is played through a door that is actually a one-way mirror. The person outside can be studied and evaluated without being embarrassed. Since NYNY is a membership club, those who are unwelcome, or who do not fit the mix for the evening, are simply not invited in.

But how do you find out how to fit the mix?

"The game is developing a presence, a look," says William Pitt, III, a disco authority and consultant, and spokesman for New York New York.

"You want to look interesting, exciting, like you can contribute something to the act. When you understand that it's the people who really create the ambiance, you realize that the door game isn't all that snobbish or superficial. Everybody is part of a big performance, and everybody has to contribute."

Pitt, who created the new social-climber game called "Social Scandal," designed by Milton Bradley, says that crashing a disco door is pretty much like crashing a social set. He has devised the following set of tips for would-be discogoers: ten great ways to crash a tough door.

How to Play the Door Game and Win—Maybe

"There has been a great deal of publicity about the *terror* of the door at the better-known discotheques. The elitism and selectivity have made more than just the common man angry. Movie stars, politicians, and some of the world's most wealthy people have been turned away at the doors, so don't be too upset when—or if—it happens to you."—WILLIAM PITT

1. *Be beautiful.* This is the master key that will unlock any disco door in the country. A careful and intelligent selection of parents and genes is an essential. Being born a beautiful person will open doors for you anywhere—not only at discotheques. Score 100 points. You're in.

2. *Be stylish.* High fashion works. Dress up to the highest standards of *Vogue* magazine or *Gentlemen's Quarterly.* (Study the fashion sketches in this book for the Five Dominant Disco Looks.) Be careful of heavy looks and overdressed

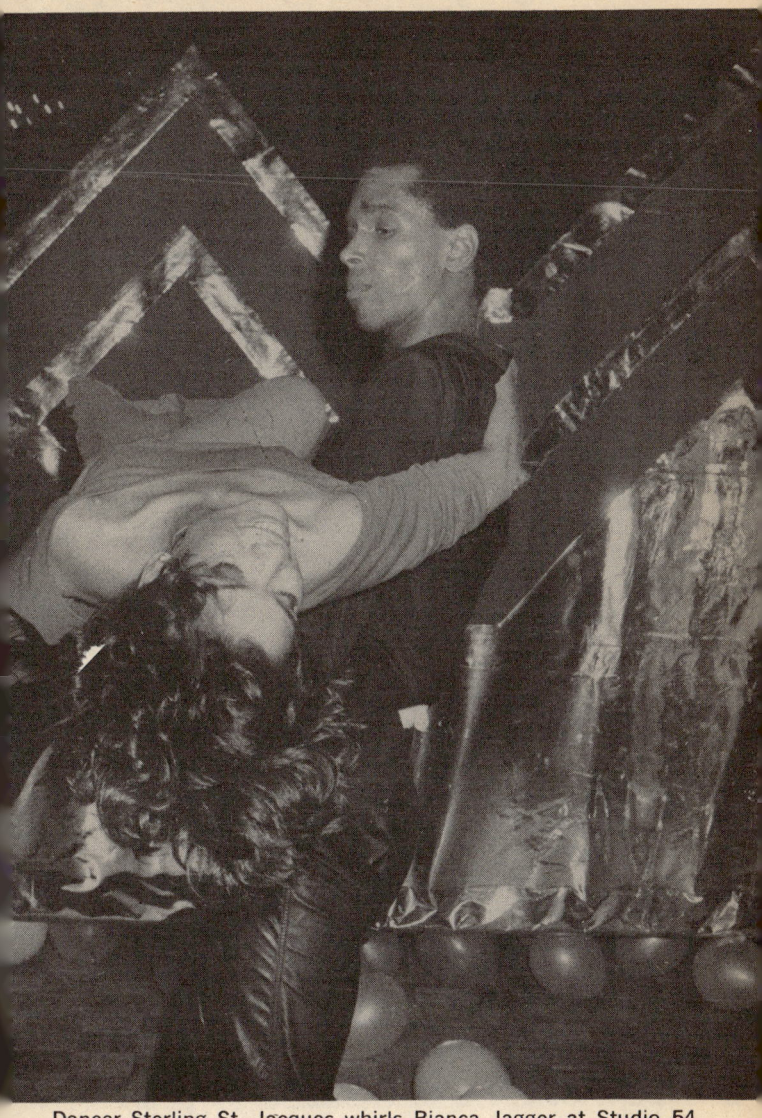

Dancer Sterling St. Jacques whirls Bianca Jagger at Studio 54
NEW YORK DAILY NEWS PHOTO

Jacqueline Bissett and photographer Scavullo at Studio 54
NEW YORK DAILY NEWS PHOTO

Regine's, 502 Park Avenue, New York City

A very chic place for the very rich and famous who go there to see (and be seen by) the very rich and famous. Once you step inside this glittering fantasy club, you begin to understand why Regine is known as the Queen of the Discos. The chic is very international, and the Art Deco room is a-glitter with star-type celebrities from the world of business, politics, fashion, and entertainment. Beautifully dressed, beautiful-looking people move on and off the lighted plexiglass floor, where the music is a mix of hard and mellow disco. This is no place to go if you're on a budget, and dinner for two in the restaurant can easily cost you $100. Three glasses of Perrier water and one Drambuie cost one couple more than $32—and that was in addition to the admission which runs around $12 apiece. Reservations are required, and so are jackets for men and "evening elegance" for women. The seating around the dance floor in the disco is in circular banquettes centered by tiny round coffee tables, and unless you go with a group, you may find yourself cheek-to-chic with strangers who are as disappointed that *you* aren't a celebrity as *you* are that *they're* not. The food in the restaurant is good, and if you can afford it—and the door people let you in—it's fun to go at least once, just to be able to say you did. When Regine herself is *en scène*, the place zings!

New York New York, 33 West 52nd Street, New York City

This has been called possibly the most beautiful disco in the world. A great-looking, great-sounding disco, you can go back here often for the sophisticated decor, the unusual special effects, the light show of neon and spotlights and laser beams. Designer Angelo Donghia's gray flannel walls and Chinese red lacquer surfaces and lots of glass and polished metal give this disco a super-cool look. There's an elegant outer lounge for rest and recuperation and socializing, and comfortable banquettes around the floor where you can sip a drink and watch the action. You won't watch for long, though, for the deejay puts together music that pulls dancers onto the floor and keeps them there. There's a mirrored bar with lilac neon light sculptures that seem to float over the heads of the bartenders.

Design Circuit, Inc., of New York City, which has designed some of the most famous nightspots in the world, is responsible for the special effects that run riot with laser beam lighting, neon bolts, and revolving spotlights—and the most spectacular experience of the evening—a mist that begins to rise from the floor as fountains of smoke pour from the ceiling, and you find yourself dancing in an eerie, other-world of disembodied spirits. This disco is located in the famed old Toots Shor restaurant, and in September of 1978, its owners will have ready for the public a new restaurant upstairs along with a cabaret theater. All this and disco, too.

Visitors here include the likes of Warren Beatty, Gregory Peck, Ben Vereen, Norman Mailer, Robert Duvall, and a crowd of good-looking young urbanites. Nonmembers admitted when there is room.

★★

"If anything, disco is the great leveler," says Sari Becker, an executive of RSO Records' New York office. "At 54, for instance, you can find Bianca Jagger or Margaret Trudeau dancing with the bus boys."

★★

Infinity, 633 Broadway, between Third and Bleecker Streets, New York City

If you could visit only one discotheque in your life, Infinity should be it. It is more than a discotheque, it is a mindblowing experience, a wild, intense, and spaced-out affair that seems to be the very essence of disco. This one-time factory on lower Broadway has a block-long dance floor, and all those writhing, leaping bodies you see out there aren't reflections in mirrors, as they are in so many discos. Those are real people, and they really are dancing all the way back to the next block! The floor is a mass of dancing figures. People dance on the

Bianca Jagger, Mikhail Baryshnikov, Mick Jagger, Alana Hamilton at Bianca's birthday party at Studio 54

NEW YORK DAILY NEWS PHOTO

ledges of huge mirrored arches, on the pedestals of the Gothic pillars that soar to the black ceiling, in the lounges, around the bar. Wherever there is a flat surface at Infinity, someone is sure to be dancing on it.

There are speakers, speakers everywhere, and Jim Burgess, the disc jockey, is considered by some to be the best in the country now spinning in a club. He and his light man have one of the most creative lighting and sound systems in the country to play with. This discotheque was the first to be lighted with neon, and the effect is an intense kind of solid light that flashes, whirls, runs across the ceiling, plunges down the walls, whips and spins around the pillars. Neon arches around the windows flash on and off in time to the music, and dancers shout and sing along and howl joyously when the place goes dark and the strobe lights turn everything into spastic slow motion.

There are bars to refresh the thirsty, and huge bowls of energy food—fruit, nuts-and-raisins, potato chips, and chocolates—sit around for free refueling. The crowd is young, middle class, and blue collar, and you'll find a lavish spicing of fantasy folk and masqueraders here, along with an occasional celebrity or two.

Infinity is still hot long after other hot spots have cooled, and you shouldn't be surprised to see a line waiting to get in at five in the morning, when the bar is closed but the dance goes on. This disco is only open on Fridays and Saturdays, from 11 P.M. on. Nonmembers admitted when there is room.

Odyssey 2001, Bay Ridge, Brooklyn, New York

This is the disco made famous by *Saturday Night Fever*, filmed in this neighborhood club which has been around for some thirty years, and has recently gone disco. Odyssey did not look the way you saw it in *Fever* when the Robert Stigwood Organization people first appeared to case the place and talk about making a movie there. It was spruced up considerably for the film, chief spruce being the underlit dance floor which Lite-Lab of New York manufactured for the film, and

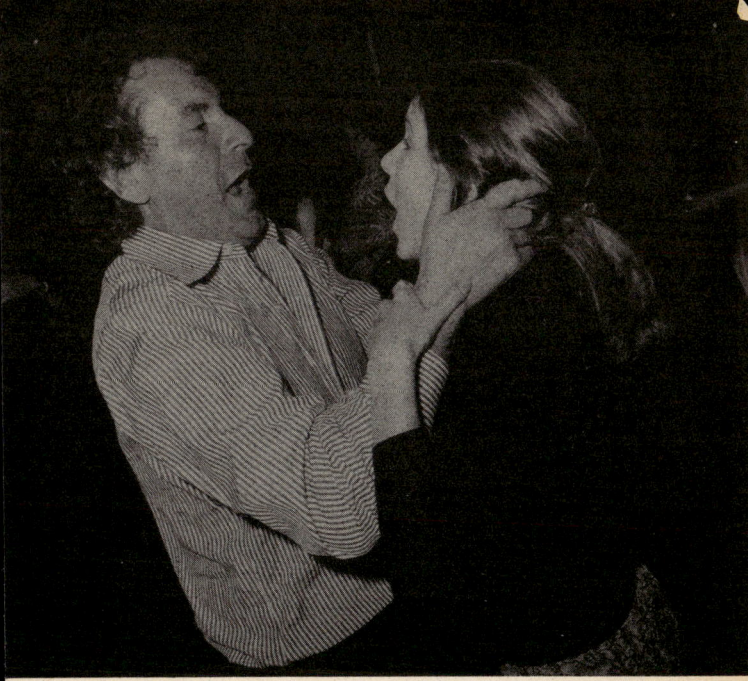

Milos Foreman and Carrie Fisher do a "punk" dance at New York New York   NEW YORK DAILY NEWS PHOTO

on which Travolta performed so spectacularly. When the movie people pulled out, they still owed the disco owners some $15,000 for miscellaneous expenses, including the loss of business for six weeks while the disco was closed for filming. To settle the debt, Paramount Pictures left the floor and the lights, so you will see them if you drop in.

The disco owners and the neighborhood people have mixed feelings about the film, which they say did not truly represent the life-style of the area. On the other hand, business at the club has improved nearly 100 percent, and a lot of people picked up an easy $68 a day for work as extras. Odyssey may not sparkle as it did in the film, but for the young men and women who go there, it's still a popular place to dance.

La Main Bleue, Paris, France

In Paris, Regine, who has been the unchallenged queen of nightlife for more years than most women like to count, is being given a run for her disco money by a disco that is Europe's biggest dance hall—La Main Bleue, The Blue Hand.

Buried like a raw concrete warehouse in the bowels of a (then) half-finished suburban shopping center, this new "disco hot" was once just 1,300 square feet of space that nobody wanted out in the Montreuil area of Paris. Its bleak decor was so ugly that the owner, Jean Michel Moulhac, had it painted in black tarmac "as an improvement," and brought in laser lights to boost the existing mauve neon tubes.

Moulhac bought the warehouse and designed the disco to provide a dance and music club for black immigrant workers in Paris.

"Even when they are accepted elsewhere, they can't afford the prices," explains the owner, who offers dancers $2 drinks and nonstop music. It was to be a place where French-speaking Africans and West Indians could meet and dance. The first surprise was the way gypsies turned up from the squatter encampments around Paris to join the fun and spice the ambiance.

Before long; the quality of the music, the dancing, and the steam bath atmosphere began to lure all of Paris and international society, the way that Harlem once drew chic New Yorkers in the forties. Before you could say "fever," Saturday night at La Main Bleue became the chic night. Such after-dark nightlifers as the Yves St. Laurent people, the *Vogue* magazine crowd, top fashion models and photographers, designers with their p.r. men, show up on chic night to see, be seen—and actually dance.

The fashion parade is almost as much of an attraction as the music and the dancing, for the regulars at the disco really turn it out. They show up in sensational outfits, many of them borrowed from old American musicals, with a heavy emphasis on the zoot suit. Lapels are embroidered, spangled, or beaded, pants are hitched to high waists, and red satin neckties hang out like a thousand panting tongues.

High point of the evening is something straight out of John Travolta's film. At 2 A.M., the disco jockey, dressed in silver pants, silver vest next to the skin, and wearing a silver cap, stops the action on the floor to call forward the best ten male dancers spotted during the evening. One at a time, each does a solo dance routine with all the stops pulled out, until a winner is chosen by a public applause meter. He gets a hi-fi stereo rig instead of a cup; then everyone goes back to dancing until it's time to catch the first morning Metro train home at 5 A.M.

★★

"There is nothing so necessary to human beings as the dance . . . without the dance, a man would not be able to do anything. All the misfortunes of man, all the reverses with which histories are filled, the blunders of politicians and the failures of great leaders—all this is the result of not knowing how to dance."

The author of these solemn words sound like a 1970s discophile—but he was a 1670s French dancing master.

★★

Civic Theatre Discotheque, New Orleans, Louisiana

Located in one of the city's most historic entertainment landmarks, this disco has all the excitement of Infinity in New York, although on a smaller scale, with a great deejay perched high above the stage which is now the dance floor. This is the largest and most popular disco in New Orleans. The Shuberts built the theater as a playhouse in 1904. Since then, it's been an opera house, a movie house, and a burlesque theater. The orchestra and box seats were torn out to make room for white tables and metal chairs. In the lower balcony, there are no tables or chairs, only cushions on the floors. There are five bars—one of them in the former orchestra pit. There's also a celebrity bar, a room at the back of the theater where the walls are covered with photographs of artists and stars who have performed here. Renovation cost more than a quarter of a million dollars, and if you've ever danced at this disco, you'll say it was worth it. There's a lot of good dancing and a lot of good free-styling on the plexiglass dance floor of the stage where Helen Hayes and Tallulah Bankhead once trod with much greater dignity.

Jubilation, Las Vegas, Nevada

The newest discotheque in town, this is the $3-million baby of Singer Paul Anka, named for one of his hit songs, and managed by his father, Andrew. You enter Jubilation through an airport-style metal detector, a precautionary touch that, Anka says, protects patrons from other patrons carrying guns and knives. Patrons in other discos in town have been known to become somewhat disorderly. Anka wants none of that. A couple of toters have been spotted so far and politely requested to divest themselves of their arms. So far, they have politely done so.

The 19,000-square-foot multilevel interior boasts three dining rooms overlooking the dance floor on which, from 6 to 11 P.M., conventional style dancing is the order of the evening, with a wide variety of dance music played through a discophonic sound system. At midnight, the place goes disco and goes until breakfast. Dancers from the clubs around town dance here after they're through working. The structure, of brick and glass, is built around a glass-enclosed atrium and the glass is one-way mirror from the outside. There is a room to play backgammon, four bars (including one in the lobby for the cocktail hour). Except for the disco floor, which has been specially lighted, although without the psychedelia usually associated with disco lighting, the rest of the place is illuminated by honest-to-goodness gas light. No cover. No minimum. Couples preferred. Jackets, no jeans, no T-shirts.

★★

Regine believes in high-heeled sexy shoes for dancing.
"I dance better when my feet hurt," she says.

★★

Ex-World Heavyweight Champ Leon Spinks trains and plays to the disco beat NEW YORK DAILY NEWS PHOTO

Hippopotamus: 405 East 62nd Street, New York City

Plush and sophisticated, this disco is remarkable on several counts, one being that it is one of the few survivors of the first disco wave of the sixties. The owners feel that much of that endurance record is due to Hippopotamus's having built up a loyal clientele by providing a variety of pleasures. The disco room is handsome, the sound good, and the floor always filled with a good-looking, well-dressed crowd of enthusiastic dancers. There's also an intimate restaurant with good French cooking and attentive service. There's a bar, well patronized by singles, and a backgammon room where, in the winter, you can play before a crackling fire. Reservations are a must.

Scaramouche, Miami, Florida

Described by one dancer as "an incredible place, a drug trip without drugs," this new disco is located in the posh $77-million Omni International Hotel in Miami. The setting, right out of a Rafael Sabatini novel, is highlighted by a mind-boggling neon light wall designed by Robert Lobi of Design Circuit, Inc., in New York. It cost upward of $36,000 to put in this giant wave of neon tubing that is coolly caressing in the early evening but becomes a crashing roll of hot colors as the night goes on. The wall can be played on a keyboard that is designed to respond to the bioelectric responses of the light man, so that whatever the musical effect does to *him* results in an immediate lighting change on the floor. The wall can also be placed on auto pilot, to pulse in time with the music.

The wave of the light wall is created by thousands of colored neon tubes that run through a sheet of plexiglass positioned in front of one of the mirrored walls of the dance floor.

Bob Jones, who designed the disco, planned it as a subtly sophisticated club to appeal to today's flashy party people. It operates on sensuality, exclusivity (they really play the door game here), and membership fees.

While the light wall waves and pulses, bars of light splinter in mid-air over the disco floor, and tiny mirror balls spit kaleidoscopic images all over the place, and finally, billows of colored fog blur the dancers to the waist as they move.

Both the free-form bar and the dance floor are made of polished Travertine marble, and imported Italian chrome and brass tables furnish the backgammon room that overlooks the lounge and the dance floor. The lamps near the seating areas look like smooth boulders that glow with an unearthly light.

cent of the old French Line luxury ships. It's on designer Egon von Furstenburg's list of the "world's most beautiful discotheques."

Doubles, New York City

Located in the basement of the Sherry Netherland Hotel on Fifth Avenue, this is a private club that caters to the high society set, both local and international. It goes disco at midnight. Here, twenty- and thirty-year-olds in suits and dinner dresses dine and drink and dance in the same room with their parents and parents' friends. After the older generation departs, the young discophiles take over, but the action goes on only until about one in the morning. Doubles is often invaded late in the evening by crowds of black-tied Beautiful People coming back from charity balls and such. Scene: primarily couples. Decor: an intense red which has prompted someone to compare it to a sore throat.

The Daisy, Hollywood, California

You may be rich or famous, but unless you are a member or a guest of a member, you won't get into this exclusive discotheque in Hollywood. It's the "in" place for showbiz people to relax. Imogene Coca, who doesn't really disco, does Daisy—when she gets a chance.

El Privado, Los Angeles, California

This is a private club with $1,000 membership dues. Stars like Raquel Welch and Rod Stuart make their entrances from limousines.

Pips, Los Angeles, California

By now an old-timer as discos go—five-and-a-half years old—this is still the most elegant club in town. Members are hand-picked by the board of directors, and membership costs $1,000 plus $30 a month in dues. Couples who join sign contracts providing for a second membership at the price of the first in case their marriages break up. Caters mostly to prosperous professional types, business people, and stars of stage, screen, and television land. The disco area is casually elegant, resembling a luxurious living room. Habitués include Paul Newman, Peter Falk, Tony Curtis, Lucille Ball, Dean Martin, and Frank Sinatra.

Mumms, San Francisco, California

So called because the co-owners (two pro football players) wanted a "French-type name that was easy to remember," this is a members-only disco, with membership at $300 and annual dues of $100. It's called the fizziest disco in Frisco. There's a backgammon room, and on the floor you'll find such celebrity types as Alex Haley and Patti Hearst (when she's at liberty), Mikhail Baryshnikov, and O. J. Simpson.

★★

Many of the nation's celebrities are walking around with a price on their heads—and many of them don't know it.

Bounty hunters are an important part of making a "trendy" disco happen. Club owners offer so much a head for the celebrity who is brought in.

At one time, Cher and Sylvester Stallone brought a price of $100 apiece. Alice Cooper—a little less. You can make a bonus on the bounty if your celebrity also makes the papers.

★★

If My Friends Could See Me Now

Fashion designers call it a return to elegance. Fashion photographers declare it's the only style worth snapping a shutter at. Sociologists say it's a reflection of the new participation-and-movement culture of the seventies. It's disco fashion, disco dressing, and it's the hottest thing in the fashion field today.

After years of dedication to the casual blue-jean look, people are dressing up again. Nights of quiet stay-at-home parties are out. Going out is in. Dancing is what has made it happen, and clothes to dance in have become the trademark of the new American night-life style. More and more people are finding that dressing for disco gives them a chance to change not only their clothes but their personalities as well, and they are turning themselves out in styles that are chic, sexy, exciting, outrageous—and most of all, different. Discos are a flight into fantasy, and disco fashion is the boarding pass.

There are five so-called dominant looks on the disco fashion scene today, and Rita Hamilton, Fashion Editor of the *Daily News Record*, a Fairchild publication, has prepared a handbook of disco dressing, discussing the do's, don'ts, and musts of these five important looks. The accompanying sketches were prepared by Robert Melendez, who, for the past ten years, has been an illustrator with *Women's Wear Daily*.

When it comes to disco dressing, the adage "the best things in life are free" certainly holds true. The best—in fact, the *only*—clothes for serious dancing must be free, loose, and comfortable. Fashion designers themselves abandon excess apparel when they go disco dancing, and most of them prefer comfortable clothes that they can layer and then peel off as the evening goes on.

Dressing is very much an essential part of the whole disco

phenomenon, and discotheques have become parade grounds for fashion voyeurs. However, what is appropriate for one disco may be grossly inappropriate for another. So before you choose your outfit, think out where you are going, what the crowd will be like, and what image you want to project. A navy blazer with khaki or gray flannel pants is the safest look for a man, while a flimsy blouse, vest, and big skirt will work for his partner. Both looks will fit easily into a disco crowd in Manhattan—or in the Midwest.

But before you settle on the better-safe-than-sorry route, remember, you are going dancing to have fun. And having fun with your clothes is a natural extension of the mood you want to project.

Try to wear amusing sportswear whenever you can. The clothing style will subtly transfer itself to your dancing style. Amusement, light-heartedness can transform men's wear into a terrific women's look for disco dancing. Try such touches as skinny ties, small-collared blouses, vests, flopping, oversized jackets teamed with tight pants.

Conversely, men should avoid the suit look whenever possible. Disco clothes should never ever be the same outfit you would wear to the office. Choose casual sportswear separates, instead.

There are really very few rigid rules when it comes to disco dressing, but there are some legitimate guidelines, and they are similar for men and women.

1. Wear something light. Something cool. Disco dancing is hot work.

2. Avoid tight or constricting clothes. Disco dancing is a strenuous physical activity and it requires loose and comfortable apparel. (Professional dancers say there is no need to forego tight-fitting or form-fitting costumes as long as the fabric stretches with you.)

3. Disco snobs divide the world into the silk-and-cotton crowd, the Qiana crowd, and the polyester crowd. But it does make sense to avoid synthetic fibers in the clothes you wear to go dancing. Synthetics look good, but they retain perspiration, and that looks bad on the dance floor. Actually, the same is true of silks—regardless of their snob appeal. Wear silks for looking, but not for dancing.

4. Adopt an easier attitude toward clothing. Consider looks

you wouldn't normally wear. It's a time for fun—in your clothes and on the floor.

5. Avoid the John Travolta look. It was on the way out in chic clubs even before the movie *Saturday Night Fever* hit the screens. (Last May, three-piece white suits were selling like hotcakes from Brooklyn to Los Angeles and department store managers weren't able to keep the outfit—including the black shirts and Cuban heels—in stock. If you didn't succumb then, don't. It's the most perishable look on the disco scene.)

6. Forego the pukka shells and heavy gold jewelry. They are both passé by now. In jewelry this season, less is more.

7. Get rid of all those glitter or day-glo clothes. They don't work any more. Disco dressing definitely needs shine and dazzle, but now you should be adding it through exaggerated makeup and glittery accessories—never through your clothes.

8. Never, never, never wear a slogan T-shirt.

9. Carry a prop. In touch dancing, your hands are engaged with your partner. But free-style disco dancing leaves your hands free. Carry a fan for a sultry Carmen Miranda touch. Wear sunglasses to set you off. Carry big squares of fabric to swirl around as you spin. Wear a muffler—or carry a tambourine. Even your hair can give you something to play with while you are dancing. The main point is, have fun with your accessories.

10. Don't try too hard. Being comfortable inside your own skin carries more fashion clout than all the Pucci, Gucci, and Fiorucci put together.

★★★

Diaper dresses are fashion designer Norma Kamali's contribution to the disco scene, and not only do they look sexy, they make sense.

"They free the dancers' legs like a swimsuit does," she notes. The "diapers" come in everything from silk to terry cloth, but they still bear a strong resemblance to the original "three-cornered pants."

★★★

Do-It-Yourself Disco Tips

Some of the most interesting "looks" that show up at discos around the country can easily be put together with items most women already have. A young woman at New York City's Studio 54, for example, wore basketball shorts, a T-shirt—and then gathered around herself about three yards of sheer gauze fabric—to create a really super, womanly look. That may be a bit extreme, but there are other tricks to homemade disco chic. Raid the closet, raid your mother's closet, clean up the attic, and visit the local thrift shop. Add a little imagination to what you find—and create a lot of excitement:

*Update the anklet look by pinning a cameo or some other kind of pin on the sock, just where it folds.

*Take an old long strand of pearls—or other interesting-looking beads—attach a little paper wallet to it for your money and keys, and sling the whole thing across your chest.

*Buy a fistful of colored diaper pins, or steal them from your favorite baby, and use them to attach scarves and handkerchiefs.

*Stock up on yards of big silk ribbons in all colors and use them to attach keys or bags or fans, by wrapping them around your waist.

*Slip a sheer shirt over tube tops or leotards.

*Make your own skirt or tunic top by draping three yards of fabric around yourself, fasten the sides with ribbons or pins.

*Update your last-season's pants by drawing them in at the bottom with fancy colorful ribbons and bows.

*Brighten up your sneakers with dyed laces.

*Crochet your own disco bag.

*Poke around in departments and shops devoted to dancers' clothes. Some of disco's best styles (like the leotards) are borrowed from dance clothes. Dancers' leg warmers have been seen in discos for several seasons, but they still can add a knockout touch to an ensemble.

FASHION SKETCHES BY ROBERT MELENDEZ

High Cafe Society (or monied merchandise)

The word for this kind of disco fashion is soft and sexy, but the quality of the design—as well as the price tag—must shine through. Otherwise, you've missed the point. Often, he is wearing a three-piece suit in which the jacket does not match the vest and pants—which *do* match. She may be in flounced designer dresses or seductive evening pajamas, and her primary prop, in this case, is a big scarf. Again, exaggeration is the important look. Filmy chiffon-y dresses or strapless tops are also right for the big night out.

The Studio Set

They are called core people because they form the glittery, fashion-y, café society chic-erie that you'll find as regulars at discos like Manhattan's Studio 54, or perhaps Zorine's in Chicago.

Core people go to be seen as well as to dance. When the cool weather hits, he'll be wearing loose, easy sportswear separates that he can strip off as the evening progresses. She'll be soft and slinky in a tunic top and pants. Here, she wears a tank-top slink, two disco bags for exaggeration, frizzy hair, and earrings. He has a skinny tie, button-down shirt—and that very very small collar is pure Brooks Brothers exaggeration.

The sleeves are rolled up and the lapel is pulled up—almost standing. The pants are pleated—almost all of men's pants will be pleated this fall and winter.

The girl, wearing a jacket fourteen times too big for her, with a clutch under her arm, and pegged pants, looks just right. Rings and things and high heels are still "it" in discos, and so are the little socks.

★★

The big rage among disco devotees—at least, those with a little money to spend—are gold and diamond fingernails. These are applied, firmly it is to be hoped, over the wearer's own nail.

Ten and 14-karat gold nails run $350 for the set; $35 for one.

One gold nail set with pavé diamonds sells for from $285 to $435.

★★

Macho Man and Pretty Baby (or Travolta Revisited)

This shows him without the jacket of his famous three-piece suit, and in layered looks. Again, the clothes are up-size and loose. For this look, wear a small-collared shirt, a T-shirt underneath, and carry a tambourine.

Muscles are optional.

Pretty Baby is wearing a big, mesh, oversized European-look sweater and tight peg pants—actually blue jeans. Ankle socks, of course.

(Although these are the looks you'll see most, there is still room for the sexy kind of slinky Saturday Night dress, too. Upper Right. Note her cap.)

Note: The man's coat sleeves are pushed up. The idea is to appear that you're so casual about a good suit that you'll roll up the sleeves and push them up. (It's the same principle as trailing your mink on the floor.)

Fabrics are cottons, the look is always *under*dressed, as opposed to overdressed.

Annie and Andy Hall

This is the here, there, and everywhere look that is a safe bet this fall and winter, no matter where your dancing feet take you.

He is wearing a shirt with a band collar . . . skinny tie knotted very loosely . . . and oversized jacket and oversized pants.

She's got on a boxy jacket—again, "*over*sized" is the word. That hunter safari hat on frizzy permanented hair is great and so are the high heels and big skirt.

This look is safe to wear everywhere.

The new proportion is BIG—big casual separates with small-collar shirts, skinny ties, and oversized jackets. Natural fibers and textured rough fabrics are best.

Body Beautiful Look

This is the look for disco at resorts or if it is warm where you are. Here the mood is again oversized and easy. You should look as if you had come directly off the beach to the disco floor, without hours of preparation first. (Of course, it takes hours of preparation to achieve the look.)

This athletes-show-off look involves lots of drawstrings, big shirts, shorts, and lots of exposed skin for him and her.

She is wearing high heels and bobby sox. He's wearing sandals. The girl on the right is in a flimsy sheer fabric—and he is wearing overalls. The girl on the left flings a big rectangle of fabric around.

Frizzy hair is great. Lots of bracelets are great.

Our "jock" is in a flowered shirt and drawstring pants, with jacket open—always worn open. A baseball caps adds the final touch.

Our jock-ette wears combs in her hair. The girl at the left wearing shorts, bra top, and flowered shirt that she might have snitched from her boyfriend is in perfect "taste" for this dance floor. Notice her tiny little disco bag.

The idea is always to show off the body beautiful. Tans are a must.

Women's disco clothes, says designer Stephen Burrows, should be easy-moving, a little sexy, a little alluring, and in a style that is mostly bare and keeps the arms free. His disco dresses are short, he says, because "they keep your legs free."

Burrows, who spends five or six nights a week in discotheques and dances hard and long ("It's virtually the only exercise I get"), recommends "bright colors, metallics or prints—things that can hold up under the lights."

And wear high heels with those short dresses, he adds. Your feet won't hurt if you remember to come down on your toes instead of your heels.

Foot Fashion

From the top of her frizzy head to the tip of her toes, this season's chic disco dancer will glitter. The razzle-dazzle that has already sparked disco accessories—combs, makeup, skin-sparkle—will make a big splash in shoes, as well. The slippy, drapey dresses and the ankle-hugging pants have put a new emphasis on shoes.

In discos everywhere, they will be dancing atop high, strippy, and undeniably sexy sandals. Slings, slides, and insteps will be the most popular, and they will be seen in gleaming metallics of bronze and gunmetal, shiny satins and patents. There will be rhinestones, bugle beads, and sequins on heels, straps, and vamps.

For dancers who want comfort along with their exercise, there will be ballet slippers of glitter-cloth, or vividly colored satin sneakers.

Boots will continue to be big—but perhaps not as high. This year's disco boot is more likely to be the short, fringed, or cowboy boot. Tuck the pants inside.

Sneakers of shiny satin come in a variety of lustrous colors
I. MILLER

The ultimate disco sandal . . . a towering heel with ties that wrap sexily around the ankle
DELMAN SHOE SALON

This low fringed boot worn over pants is the perfect look for disco dressing
DELMAN SHOE SALON

Do-It-Yourself Disco Dressing

PINS: Lapel pins are great accessories this year for both men and women. Wear faces and stickpins and flowers and butterflies, as many and as much as your lapel can hold. You may even wear authentic World War II insignia for the military look. This is a good look for daytime, too, but don't wear as

48

many—no more than six. If there's a war veteran in the family, you're in fashion luck.

CAPS: Any kind of cap is good on the dance floor—for men as well as women. It keeps your hair from getting into too much of a mess while dancing, and it's a perfect topping look. This one is for her—the Newsboy cap and the "Philip Morris" bellhop special.

FANS: This is obviously a fashion accessory that is functional as well as chic—and fun. That room does get warm after a few hours of dancing. That face-mask fan is good because nighttime is a time for exaggeration. You can make it yourself out of papier-mâché. And don't forget to make up your fan when you make up your face!

DISCO BAGS: You don't really wear all four at once, but this shows a variety. One is a little paper wallet that you can pick up at any notion counter or dime store . . . a tiny rolled bag looks good . . . a crocheted bag that you can make yourself on a dateless evening . . . or you can attach any small bag to an old long strand of beads and fling them over your shoulder.

COMBS: Exaggerate the look of combs. Apply your own glitter . . . You can pick up the ingredients at any dime store.

RIBBONS: Ribbons, ribbons everywhere. You wear them in your hair, on your arms and ankles . . . use them as ties for your sneakers or for lace-up shoes and sandals.

The Disco Doll is wearing an inexpensive dancers' leotard in a flesh tone, both top and bottom. Over this she has draped a square of fabric—about two and a half yards—and has added little ribbons on both sides and made it into a tunic. (Haunt the remnant counters, and you may find some really fabulous fabrics for practically pennies. Look for polka dots. Little polka dots are very big in discos now.)

Note the fan, the bracelet, the earrings, the bracelet, the ribbons—and bracelet. Hair is pulled back under a bellhop Philip Morris cap. The glittery shoes have high heels, and on the socks, on one ankle, she has attached a small cameo to the fold.

Makeup for the Disco Face

Disco lights are harsh. Normal makeup procedures often leave women looking pale and wallflowerish. The natural look that is so great on the street is pasty on the dance floor. To avoid this washed-out look, there are three key elements to remember when applying makeup before a disco evening:

1. *Exaggerate*. Outline your eyes with crayon, with the shadow applied more severely than you would for daytime. Heavy mascara is necessary under strobes.

2. *Define*. Outline your lips with a brown-based crayon, then apply a heavier coat of lipstick and gloss.

3. *Reconstruct*. Reshape your face, your cheekbones, and you chin with a darker base. This is the time to bring out all the Hollywood in you. The general rule is to apply a cream base with a slightly darker powder touched over it.

The Disco Perm

The permanent-wave hairdo is the most functional hairdo for disco. For evening, it can be blown-out with a hair dryer, or you can let it dry naturally into the kinks, unset. There are three good looks: One is to let it go natural, one is to brush it off to the side, and the third is to have it more tightly controlled, either braided with little wisps hanging around, or a little bun in the back.

Fashion Designers

You won't pick them out in a disco crowd.

The men and women who bring new fashions to the forefront are least likely to be seen wearing "the latest thing" when they go out disco dancing. The "patriarchs" of the American fashion community, like Bill Blass and John Weitz, will probably be wearing a natty blue blazer and camel or gray flannel slacks. Others of the "new breed," like Calvin Klein, Charles Suppon, or Charlie Ellis, are likely to be seen in cowboy boots, T-shirts, and jeans.

It is fashionable in the designer community to underdress, and Egon von Furstenburg, who now designs men's clothes, explains the phenomenon:

"We like the casual look. When you look at clothes all day, you want to simplify at night."

Von Furstenburg, author of *The Power Look*, a recently published encyclopedia for men, devotes an entire chapter to disco dressing, which, he says, will become increasingly important in the fashion scene.

"More and more people are coming down with the Saturday Night Fever, and the gap between daytime dressing and nighttime dressing is widening. There is one look for business and daytime—what I call 'the power look.' It's conservative—suit, tie—everything that reflects an image of confidence and authority.

"But at discos, you can be yourself. People are dressing more and more for themselves these days, and that's healthy."

For the disco dancer he suggests such "looks" as:

*Tweedy—casual yet classy
*Black on black—in any combination
*Blouson or no-collar shirts
*Touches—like dark glasses and gloves
*Most important: create an image, don't simply follow fashion.

British designer Hardy Amies is dressmaker to the Queen of England, couturier to international society, and style setter for the international male. He also is a disco freak.

"Discotheques," he says, "are the one place in which I wish I were fifty years younger—but also the one place where I'm so high that I don't give a damn.

"From my experience, discotheques are a far healthier experience than the old nightclubs. You don't sit around smoking the wrong things and drinking too much, and if you do drink, in a discotheque you work it off on the dance floor.

"My favorite disco is New York New York in, of course, New York. It is a little more intimate, and everyone just lets go. And in a disco, it's essential that everyone participate. Everyone must dance. And when you dance, you shouldn't give a damn what you look like or what you're doing or who you're dancing with. A disco is a free-for-all!"

Amies's fashion advice for the disco dancer is the philosophical advice that he applies to all fashion:

"A man should look as if he had bought his clothes with intelligence, put them on with care, and then forgotten all about them."

Men's Fashion—Cheap Chic

"Disco nights needn't be expensive," says Henry Post, a confirmed discophile and author of *The Ultimate Man*, a roundup of inside information on everything from diet to plastic surgery, from hair transplants to the art of dressing. For the disco nut who has more enthusiasm than hard cash, Post offers some pointers on cheap chic.

"Thrift shops across the country can supply you with cheap disco fashion that is easy to wear and wears well. Pick up a combination nylon-seersucker sports shirt of the type popular in California in the 1950s—about $8."

"White linen and pleated trousers, especially cut, should run about $20."

"Look for an Art Deco man's rayon scarf, and hunt for women's shoes of the 50s. They're right in style again."

"Army surplus is great for dancing. If an army can fight a war in an outfit, you can be sure to last through the night in it. Army surplus is both handsome and high in quality. Almost any military clothing can look great when it is pulled out of its former context and worn in a disco. Let your imagination go. It's inexpensive and fun."

"Disco fashion should be fun and easy, unless it's very formal. Pick clothing that moves as well as you do. If you wear a jacket, flip the collar of the polo shirt up and out. The trick is to make the conservative look appear relaxed and natural, as if you've just come from a friend's dinner party and are wound up and ready to go."

Jean Chic

Blue jeans—good old American denim—still make up one of the hottest fashion looks in today's discotheques. The chic trick is to wear them with pizzazz. And that, says Jerry Hart of New York's French Jean Store, means wearing them tight. Too tight.

"Tight jeans not only spotlight a good figure," says Jerry,

"they make the world's greatest corsets for figures that aren't so great."

Lie down to put the jeans on, pull in your stomach, and have a friend stand by to zip you up. The test of whether they are properly tight is simple, says Jerry:

"When you stand up, your eyes should pop."

Newest accessory on the disco scene are disco lashes—a totally synthetic put-on that is designed to make the wearer one with the fantasy scene. They come in turquoise, purple, pink, silver, and gold.

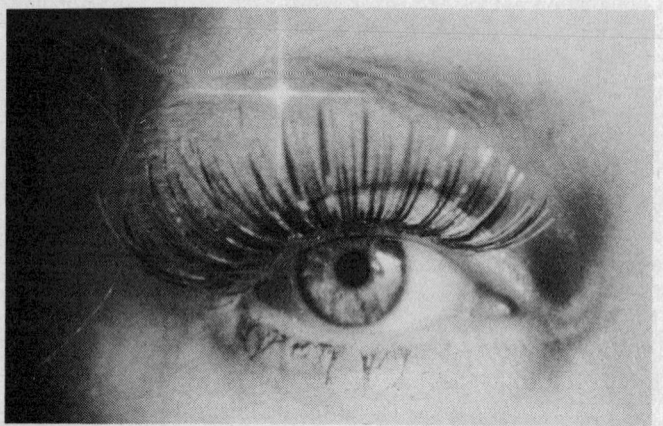

"Sue's Eye" wearing disco lashes   ANDREW YALE

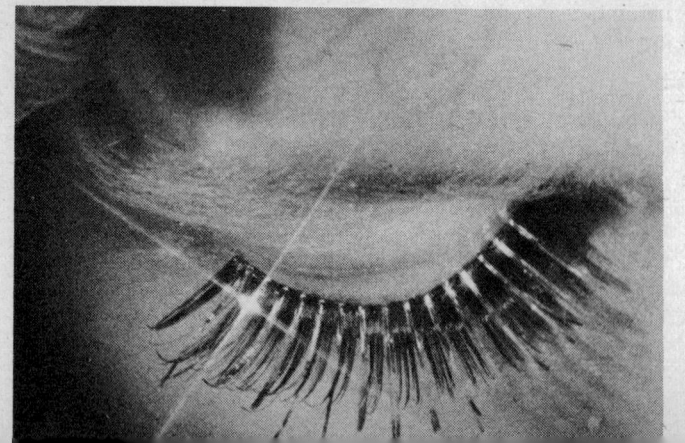

Putting the best disco foot forward with "Original Toerings"
TOERINGS LTD.

With sandals *in*, and toes *out*, a New York firm, called the Original Toerings, Ltd., has come out with a line of sterling silver and 14-karat gold rings—to be worn on the toes, not the fingers. They are specially designed to fit toes of any size and can be worn two or three to a toe. For weddings and engagements, they can be ordered with diamonds.

Stayin' Alive

Much has been said about the psychological values of disco dancing as an emotional releaser of tensions and a catharsis for the acting-out of fantasy. But disco dancing can also be good for your physical health. It stretches some muscles, strengthens others, and gives your heart and lungs—your entire circulatory system—a terrific workout. But don't forget, especially if you are just getting into the scene, that despite all the dressy clothes, the music, and the sensual ambiance, disco dancing is actually a strenuous activity. Be prepared to feel some physical after-effects, especially at first.

That holds true whether your dance style is super-cool and creamy smooth or wild, free-form gymnastics. Caught up in the electronic beat and light-show fantastic, many office executives or filing clerks—who would never think of running a marathon or swimming the English channel—are putting themselves through strenuous endurance tests on the dance floor.

Moving or swaying or leaping around for four or five hours, nonstop, requires a flexible body and stamina.

"When I first started, I couldn't even do one of the knee bends I do in the film," says John Travolta, who executes all those turns and leaps on the screen so easily. "I couldn't even lift myself off the floor! I needed stamina I didn't have.

"So I hired the boxer who trained Sylvester Stallone for *Rocky* and I went into training for five months, dancing three hours a day and running two miles a day. By the end of five months, I had lost twenty pounds and I had a whole new body."

That boxer was Jimmy Gambina, who used to handle professional fighters before working as a stunt double. As a trainer, he made Sly Stallone a "boxer" and gave John Travolta the stamina of a disco king.

Exercises

These exercises were especially designed for disco dancing by James Bourne, former ballet dancer, now of the Bourne Exercise Studio in Scarsdale, New York.

Bourne's exercises employ the principles of stretching and strengthening that develop stamina and, at the same time, help bodies achieve flexibility. The philosophy on which these designed-for-disco exercises are based allows people of all ages to participate and disco to capacity.

Exercise #1: Strengthens muscles in feet, stretches calves and backs of legs, improves balance.

Start with the "basic posture," standing erect, eyes front, hands at side, feet apart six inches.

Bend the knees slowly forward so they are directly over the toes. Lift the heels off the floor, pressing them forward. Straighten the knees, slowly balancing for a moment on your toes before lowering the heels to the floor.

Repeat five times. You'll especially appreciate this one if you are a wearer of high heels, for it makes dancers more comfortable, chiefly because when you are wearing high heels you wind up dancing on your toes or the balls of your feet.

Exercise #2: Develops strength in thighs and around the knee joint. Improves flexibility of legs, knees, and hips. Stretches lower back muscles.

Start in the "basic posture." Begin by bringing the right knee to the chest with the fingers laced together on the knee, pressing the knee to the chest.

Hold that position for three slow counts.

Slowly lower the foot to the floor.

Repeat four times with each leg.

Anything that lifts the legs is good exercise, and this will prepare you for any disco move that involves bending the knees.

Exercise #3: Tightens buttocks and abdomen. Increases

mobility of hips and upper body. Stretches lower back.

Start in "basic posture." Bend the knees slightly, keeping the weight forward on the balls of your feet. In that position, arch the back, sticking the buttocks out behind you.

Then, slowly, reverse the movement by squeezing the buttocks together and tucking them underneath you.

Repeat by relaxing the buttocks, sticking them out, swaying the lower back. Repeat.

This one strengthens the lower back with a pelvic movement that builds strength and flexibility, and also looks great on the dance floor in tight jeans or a torn jersey "punk style" disco dress.

Exercise #4: Increases flexibility of upper body, firms and tones waist and torso.

Start in "basic posture." Take a wide stance with feet three feet apart, hands resting at your sides.

Weight is evenly distributed on both feet.

Shift the right hip over the right foot.

Slowly bend the upper body over to the left side, reaching with the left hand to the left ankle. Keep the body facing front as you move to the side.

Come up slowly to the center position.

Repeat on the same side five times, then change sides. This will give you plenty of flexibility and stamina for all those stepping movements of the disco dance.

Exercise #5: Stretches backs of legs, lower back, and arm muscles. Relieves tension.

Start in "basic posture." Slowly bend the knees, lowering yourself into a full squat position, placing the hands on the floor in front of you. (Keep the heels down on the floor.) Relax the head so the chin is on the chest.

Start to straighten your knees, keeping your head down and your hands on the floor. When you have straightened the legs as much as you can (you'll feel the stretching in the backs of your legs), begin to roll slowly up to an upright position.

Repeat three times.

This will stand you in good stead when the strobes start to flash and you start leaping off the floor.

Exercise #6: Builds overall stamina, balance, strength, and agility.

Stand with the right knee bent and the weight over your right foot. Point the left foot out to your side, hands on your hips for balance, then quickly, with a small jumping movement, switch legs. (Now your left knee is bent and your right foot points.)

Do this fifteen times quickly, rest a moment, then repeat.

For those of you who are very vigorous on the disco floor, Exercises #1, #3, and #5 should be done again *after* your disco dancing spree to relieve tension and prevent "post-disco soreness." This may seem a bit much to you now, and maybe even more so when you return from your night out, but they are effective. If you can muster up the courage to do them, you'll be glad you did. After you are in "disco" shape, the decision will be optional.

Being a "healthy" disco-goer may not be what you had in mind when you first came down with dancing fever. However, you will soon discover the advantages, and the difference in the way you feel—both at the discotheque and especially the day after.

Keep in mind the time and energy you devote to perfecting your disco dancing technique—constantly learning and practicing to keep on top. Think of the many steps and turns involved in devising a dynamite dance routine. Now, if you were to include exercising and eating properly in your preparation, you will begin to see how it all makes sense. As a whole, it is most certainly a discipline, but when you and your partner "shine" on that dance floor, you'll know that it is well worth it.

★★

The famous smoke-and-fog effects at New York New York, one of the country's most beautiful discotheques, was turned off, shut down, and *verboten* during the birthday party held there for Farrah Fawcett-Majors. Farrah and her husband are anti-smoking.

★★

Why We Love It

The popularity of disco, says psychologist Dr. Amitai Etzioni of Columbia University, is a reflection of the free-floating life-style of what he calls today's "untied" generation. He cites four reasons:

First: Disco dancing is free. "Free-form dancing which does not require other people or other skills makes the pleasure of dancing itself more accessible to those of us who are not as skilled and graceful. Ordinary ballroom dancing can make one feel incompetent."

Second: You don't have to touch. "Touching, in our society, seems to be a code word for intimate relationships. Group touching is all right, but one-to-one touching always is complicated."

Third: You can avoid eye contact. "Wherever you go, in New York, Hong Kong, Israel, the code is the same—no eye contact. Even if you are crowded or jostled, you can still remain private if you don't make eye contact. Eye contact seems to connote commitment."

Fourth: You don't have to have a partner. "In disco, you can dance alone, in twos, or threes—or you can dance with a surrogate partner—a chair, if you feel like it."

No Love, No Nothin'?????

Much of what goes on at discotheques works against any real sexual interaction, says psychiatrist Stuart Berger, who, at twenty-four, is probably one of the youngest shrinks in the country. Dr. Berger, currently associated with Harvard University, has been a discophile since his recent teens, and still finds time to make the disco scene.

"Disco dancing," he says, "is an extremely narcissistic exercise. Everything—the mirrors, the clothes, the volume of sound, the movement—contributes to this. There is little or no eye contact between people on the floor. They certainly can't talk to one another. People at a disco are into their own beauty, their own grace.

"The music, the dancing, gets people so into their own bodies, so involved with themselves, they don't even ask to sleep with one another!"

The ultimate goal, Dr. Berger says, is "to reach a total body experience that ruptures normal space and time."

Discos, Narcissism, and Society

(From an editorial in the New York *Daily News*)

The mania which is becoming the cultural phenomenon of the 1970s is rooted in narcissism.

Separated by walls of deafening music and swept up in a frenzy of bright lights, dancers do their own thing, seldom touching, never looking at each other, or even speaking. It's a lot like standing in front of a mirror shouting, "Me, me, me, me . . ." endlessly.

This pure self-indulgence reflects a dangerously deep-rooted philosophy in our society. It preaches that anything an individual feels like doing is 100 percent right—no matter how it affects anyone else.

The attitude shows up in our soaring divorce rate, our legions of broken families, and in countless books and movements keyed to self-gratification and self-esteem.

There is too little room for love in the philosophy that permeates the disco world. And that is a pity, for those who

★★

Elsa Martinelli, who became an international movie star in the fifties, is an international fashion designer in the seventies, and one of the world's busiest women, putting in about a fifteen-hour day.

She has no time for diets, exercises, EST, or yoga.

"My exercise is to be out at four in the morning, dancing at discotheques and sweating and drinking a lot. That's my best exercise. Then I work."

★★

have forgotten—or never known—the joys of giving and sharing are missing the richest part of life.

Narcissus

Narcissus, for those who've forgotten their *Bullfinch's Mythology*, was a gorgeous hunk of Greek, a young hunter who had never found a nymph who could really turn him on. Then one day, hungry, heated, and thirsty after a strenuous day at the bow and arrow, he came upon a beautiful spring so clear, so still, so unspoiled that it reflected the world above it like a mirror. Narcissus, leaning over to drink, saw his own reflection in the water, but being unfamiliar with mirrors, he thought that beautiful creature he saw was some lovely water-sprite, living in the spring.

He gazed at the bright eyes, the rounded cheeks, the curly locks, and the glow of health and exercise, and he fell in love. Leaning over to kiss the sprite, he plunged his arms into the water to embrace her—and immediately the image fled at his touch. Crushed with the rejection, he drew back, and after a moment, the water grew still, and the water-sprite returned again. What a tease! When Narcissus smiled, the image smiled. When he reached out his arms, the image did the same. But the moment he touched the spring—it fled.

Consumed with unrequited love, he lay on the grass and gazed upon his adored one—until he lost his color, his vigor, his beauty, and finally died. (Rumor had it that when his spirit passed over the waters of Hell's Stygian river, it leaned over to catch a look at itself.)

★★

Waist-Watchers' Hint from Fred Astaire
"To me, dancing has always been fun. It makes you look young. I mean, the very physical act of dancing is almost symbolic of youth. Dancing keeps me in good shape all year round—and I never diet."

★★

Note: Disco Dancing Can Be Good for Your Health

Dr. Maxim Asa, a noted physiologist and director of the New York Stress and Research Center, is an ex-decathlon champion on the Israel Olympics team and former chief physical fitness officer for the entire Israeli army. He is a vigorous advocate of preventive medicine through a program that combines physical fitness exercise with stress and tension release.

Here he talks about why he believes that disco dancing provides both.

Dr. Asa: I am fully in support of discos. You can quote me and I will defend it. They are a very valuable way of overriding the threshold of discomfort that usually hampers sedentary people. Exercise, in general, is not popular. For someone to really get up and do something, one must really have an incentive. It's called motivational behavior.
KH: And discos provide a motivation for exercise?
Dr. Asa: Absolutely. There is no exercise regime in any health club that can provide the motivational response that a disco does naturally. If young people and middle-aged people could actually be motivated to go into a discotheque and dance, they could increase their capacity of heart and lungs and blood pressure, and really enjoy what they are doing. It could be fantastic.
KH: Someone recently told me he has a middle-aged friend who loves disco-ing and whose slogan is "jig, don't jog."
Dr. Asa: Jogging is an excellent sport, and one should definitely indulge in it if he likes it. But jogging has become an obsession of the total population. Middle-aged people, sedentary people, they buy a pair of shoes and they jog. Some jog into coronary care units . . . and others get bitten by dogs early in the morning. I mean, the country has gone bananas as far as physical fitness is concerned, but with no direction.
KH: What brought on this physical fitness jag?
Dr. Asa: Well, you could begin with the great increase in cardiopulmonary problems in this country, and the horrendous statistics that one million adults between forty-five and sixty-five die every year because of coronary heart disease.

KH: So, how would you compare disco dancing with, say, running or jogging?

Dr. Asa: I would say that continuous disco dancing is the equivalent to running an eight- or ten-minute mile. For every ten minutes that you are continuously disco-ing, you are running a mile.

KH: So that—thing—that people do at discos is really good for them?

Dr. Asa: Absolutely. It's a super-route to cardiopulmonary fitness.

KH: You mean, this is good for my lungs?

Dr. Asa: Super, providing the atmosphere is clear. Only the pollutants in the air provide any problem. Otherwise, disco dancing is extremely good for the lungs.

KH: What does it do for my heart?

Dr. Asa: Well, it brings the heartbeat up to optimum levels and keeps it there for a long time, which increases its aerobic capacity. Disco dancing is really aerobic exercises done continuously.

KH: Aerobic means . . . ?

Dr. Asa: It means "with oxygen." Disco dancing is constantly supplying oxygen to the heart, lungs, and muscles.

KH: Can a person overdo it?

Dr. Asa: Young people don't have to watch out. But, usually, if a person feels he is overdoing it, all he has to do is stop for six seconds and check his pulse rate to see if it exceeds his optimal level—optimum, that is, for a healthy person free of symptoms.

KH: How can you tell what your optimal level is?

Dr. Asa: Generally, optimum is approximately 210 minus your age. But, let's take a safety margin and say that 200 minus one's age will constitute a comparatively safe heart rate level.

KH: So, a fifty-year-old man whose pulse reaches 150 beats per minute should stop and rest for a little while?

Dr. Asa: Yes, but if he's still at 110 or 120 with no symptoms, he can keep on dancing. Actually, one *should* exercise to the optimal level to get the full benefits.

KH: How would this compare to a game of golf, as far as exercise is concerned?

Dr. Asa: If you're talking about a golf game where you ride a cart and you have a caddy that does not even allow you to pull a club out of the bag—it's no contest. But, if you were to carry your bag and walk the hills briskly from hole to hole, it could be equivalent to an evening of disco dancing.

KH: We've been talking about all the good health aspects of disco dancing. Are there any bad features or health hazards?

Dr. Asa: Well, I may criticize the noise level and probably the effect of the decibel level that might affect some people's hearing in the future . . . There is some relationship between a degree of deafness and extended exposure to a very high sound level. And there is a chance perhaps that the oscillating lights may affect people who have hidden epilepsy. Strobe lights are, by their nature, disorienting.

KH: That's half the fun.

Dr. Asa: But that could be detrimental to some people.

KH: You said something earlier about pollutants in the air being a problem?

Dr. Asa: Yes, if the disco is a smoke-filled situation. Exercising hard in polluted air can cause problems. People with cardiac problems should never go to smoke-filled discos. Discos where the smoke is drawn off—or where smoking is not allowed—are safe.

KH: You mean, it's not the dancing that's bad for the heart?

Dr. Asa: No, no, it's the smoke. The dancing would be fantastic for them. I think that if discos really want to cash in on the health factor, they should eliminate smoking on the dance floor—and have a smoking room outside. That way, the exercise would be going on in unpolluted air.

KH: Suppose I'm just standing there, free-styling, moving my shoulders, my hips, my waist, but not really lifting my feet off the floor in any significant way. Am I getting any exercise?

Dr. Asa: Absolutely. You don't have to lift your feet, provided you bend your knees to about fifteen degrees and try to use the large muscles. You bob up and down, like in skiing. This would be sufficient to really give you the equivalent of jogging.

KH: And there's no limit to how long I can go on doing this?

Dr. Asa: There's no limitation at all. The more, the better. There is nothing more wonderful than coming home and really feeling tired in a joy of effort, and sleeping it off.

Do's and Don'ts for Surviving a Disco Night Out

Don't eat a heavy meal before you go dancing. A full stomach can make you feel sluggish, and eating before exercising is not a healthy idea, anyway. Feeling hungry, confirmed discophiles say, makes you a little hyper—and that's a better kind of high than a lot of other things around.

Nibble through the evening if you really feel hungry—just a little at a time. Many discotheques provide "energy food"—for free—bowls of chocolates, fruits, nuts, raisins, potato chips.

Do try to take a nap for several hours between leaving the job and going dancing. One of the hardest things for day people to get used to is staying up late so that they can go out to play. Disco doesn't really get going until midnight, anyway, in the cities—a little earlier in the suburbs—so you'll have time for at least four hours sleep. And it makes the waiting-around time go faster.

Don't get discouraged if you can't nap on your first couple of tries. After a few nights without much sleep, you'll do just fine.

Do allow yourself plenty of time to get dressed and ready for the night's event. Take a leisurely shower. Put on a disco record with a mellow beat (the heavy stuff comes later) and slowly immerse yourself in the mood. Listen to the music as you shampoo, shave, shower, make up. By the time you're heading out the door, you should already be dancing.

Don't use heavy perfumes, they tend to get stronger and headier as the disco beat goes on. Experienced disco-goers prefer an all-over splash of a light cologne.

Do use waterproof makeup. It doesn't slide off.

Do a few loosening-up exercises when you get home, even if it's four in the morning. They'll help you sleep and prevent post-disco soreness.

Soak your eyes and feet before hopping into bed. Apply wet (but not hot) teabags to your eyelids while you soak your feet in cool—not hot or cold—water.

Crawl into bed for another four hours' sleep.

Start your morning with a pot of coffee (for stimulation) and a high-protein breakfast with plenty of fruits for sustained energy through the day.

Take another protein break instead of coffee break to beat the three o'clock slump. A couple of tablespoons of flavored protein powder mixed with fruit juice or milk will do the trick.

★★

Worried about the possible sexual undertones (or overtones) of disco dancing? Dr. Albert Ellis, psychologist, sexpert, and author, offers this reassurance on the matter of such expressional dancing:

"There is sex implied in it, but it's not a social sex urge. There is some stimulation from the dance, but I don't believe it often leads to consummation. They must be too tired."

★★

Risky Changes

It's two o'clock in the morning, and the disco has become a steamy demiworld of leaping figures, swirling and spinning in a kaleidoscope of revolving lights that ricochet off mirror balls and mirrored walls and drench the parquet floor with pools and puddles of color.

The music that rattles my rib cage and will pound in my bloodstream long after I've gone to bed has taken the dancers to ever more-frenzied heights. We've been dancing since midnight, and the body heat has been steadily rising. My husband's necktie was the first thing to go, and I wear it as a sash around my waist and my waist is getting warm. I think longingly of being able to take off my skin and dance around in my bones. If I did, no one would notice.

A young man in saddle shoes and denims and an expensive silk shirt spins elegantly past with his partner, a life-sized female doll dressed in an identical costume and held to his feet and wrists with elastic straps. That is Mr. Christian, and he is a regular here, as is the girl who dances with a white poodle. In her arms, of course.

The young, light-skinned black man who came in with us, dressed in jacket, pants, vest, shirt and tie, and hat—with a flocked black veil wrapped around his face—moves past us for the hundredth time.

All night long, he has been dancing around the room solo, and every time he comes past, it seems, another piece of his outfit is missing. By now, he is down to shoes and jockey shorts, and it is a little nervous-making because you know he never takes off his hat and veil.

Off in the crowd you can see a white parasol moving up and down above the dancers' heads, and a few of those heads are turning. The dancer beneath the parasol is wearing nothing but a transparent plastic raincape and a garter belt and stockings. Her partner is in top hat and tails. Far across the room, a young woman in a flowing green blouse and skin-tight jersey pants is dancing solemnly with her reflection in the mirror-wall.

These are the fantasy people—the flipped side of the disco disc. These are the people who provide disco with flashes of the bizarre and touches of the outrageous with drama.

The discotheque is really an enormous stage, and all the men and women on it are not merely players—they are stars. Whatever your fantasy may be, you can act it out in a disco. Are you a mousy little secretary by day? You can be a sexy femme fatale in a disco. Do you pack groceries when the sun shines? In a disco, you can be a rock star. For a few hours a night, a couple of nights a week, you can disown your reality.

And you can do it safely, because although you are a star, with all those *other* stars around, you can at the same time be anonymous.

"That is why the crowding at discotheques is so necessary," a psychiatrist pointed out. "If you're going to do bizarre things, you like to have company, because it provides anonymity. And anonymity is essential to fantasy."

Less bizarre and not as visible are the private little fantasies of all of the hundreds of the rest of us dancing under the lights, each a part of the other's scene, yet each alone in our own private world of dreams and imagery.

Perhaps that is why we can all understand, a little, the dancer in the paratrooper uniform . . . and the man with the reddish Afro sprouting wildly above a white-feathered cat mask . . . And why people can smile at the frail and skinny boy who dances the night away in full motorcycle regalia—

★★★

Actor Roddy McDowall, who played the super-intelligent chimp in *Planet of the Apes* and an eighty-year-old gypsy crone in *Rabbit Test*, explains some of the charm of fantasy that is so much a part of the disco scene:

"It's a delight to play something very far away from one's self."

★★★

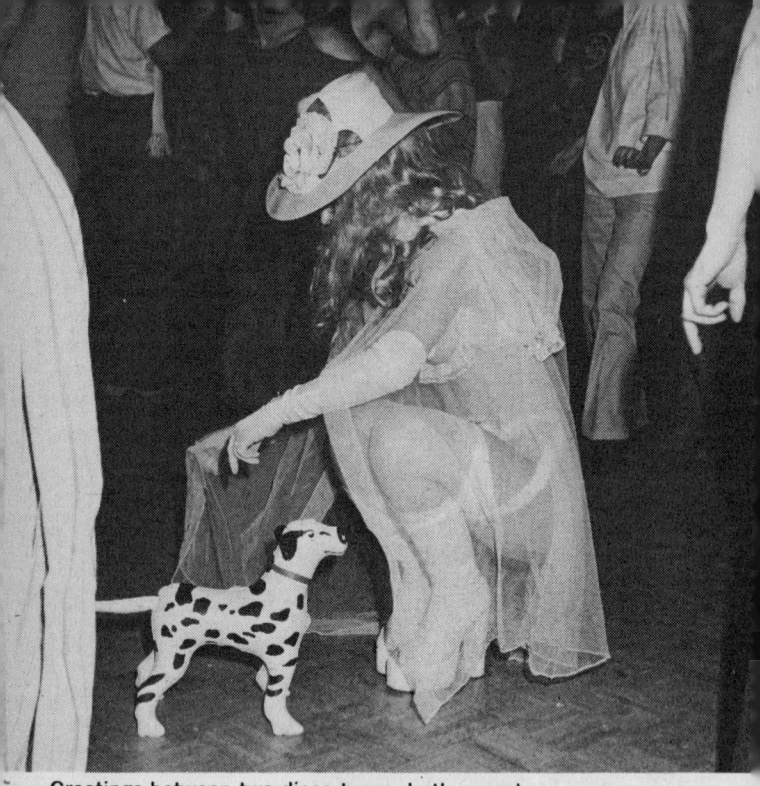

Greetings between two disco types, both unreal
1978 DISCOTHEKIN' NEWS/DOCUMENT ARCHIVES

from boots to belt to leather jacket, crash helmet, and goggles. What does it really matter if the rumpled, tweedy man who wanders around the discotheque all night with pen and sketching pad never, ever, sketches anything? Or if the beautiful dark-haired Potassa, so shapely and graceful in designer gowns, is really a man? Or that a hard-working young man who has a responsible job on Wall Street likes to dance at discotheques on roller skates in a nineteenth-century ballgown?

These are the fantasy people. The music, the lights, the dancers give the disco excitement and flavor. Fantasy gives it theater.

Le Clique

Off in one corner of the discotheque, a dark-haired young man is casually swallowing a mouthful of fire, while on another part of the floor, a clown with a painted-on grin dances with a very tall bear. A man and woman, their faces and bodies painted gleaming silver, grow amorous in the middle of the floor, while a young woman in a frenzy of dance fever literally dances herself out of her silky black disco dress.

This is not a foregathering of fantasy folk—not even a convention of crazies. It is the latest innovation on the disco scene—theatrical disco—designed to satisfy the unregenerate discophile's need for something new and different, and to satisfy the disco owners' desire to fill that need, and their cash registers as well.

It is called Le Clique, and it is a sort of traveling road show. A portable party. Sometimes, on request, almost a movable orgy. Stewart Feinstein, a fourth-grade schoolteacher, and Marlene Backer, a social worker, who created the concept, sometimes describe Le Clique as "a discotheque without walls," since, in effect, it imports fantasy and excitement into existing discotheques.

At the core of Le Clique are some thirty to forty performers recruited by Feinstein and Backer, who create the novelty and excitement that mark some of the trendier discos. It is the fantasy scene of disco multiplied, refined, exaggerated—and planned.

The idea was created out of the realization that disco audiences are a fickle bunch and can easily be lost to the next innovative competitor. To keep them coming, Le Clique creates theme parties ("Spring Prom," "Valentine's Ball," "Send in the Clones") and holds them in a variety of discotheques. Le Clique, which books the disco on its slowest night, usually Tuesday, gets a share of the money taken at the door. The disco owner gets the rest, and everything at the bar.

These are private parties, and the guests are members of Le Clique, which has an extensive mailing list. They pay the going admission rate in New York City (about $10) to attend.

When it comes to fantasy, Le Clique's performers really pile it on LE CLIQUE PHOTO

Membership dues are fairly low—$50 a year when last quoted—which puts Le Clique parties within the reach of most people. Feinstein and Backer say they are trying to avoid being "an elitist organization" which only celebrities and executives can afford, or can get into. Le Clique partygoers have the same sense of belonging that Liza Minnelli has at Studio 54.

The performers include ballet dancers, country-western singers, a professional magician and fire-eater, a porno star and friend (the Silver People), a juggler who has written, directed, and acted in films, a stripper who is a fine arts student, and a dancer who can become a statue, remaining completely immobile for as long as five hours.

Their act is not to take over the party as performers, to stop the show or the dancing, but to provide sudden, unexpected, and often startling bits of sensuality, sexuality, and fantasy.

What about those "orgies"?

"It would be hard to say if people view the parties as orgies," says Feinstein, "since there is so much going on, all night long, and in all parts of the room. The fact is that generally people tend to see what they want to see."

Disco Sally

"I gave up the law because there was no justice," says Disco Sally, seventy-eight-year-old Sally Lippman, a widow, former lawyer, and swinging darling of the crowd at Studio 54.

An accomplished Hustle dancer, Disco Sally is at the Studio seven nights a week.

Sally, who stands four-foot-ten and weighs only ninety-five pounds, is a well-spoken, quiet-voiced woman who loves to make outrageous statements on the record, and do outrageous things—like spend her nights at a discotheque in the company of an entourage of good-looking young men. Both proclivities have caused her trouble with her older brother, who, she says, feels she is making herself a laughing stock.

Unlike Vladmir Horowitz, who likes discos but puts cotton in his ears because he doesn't care for the music, Mrs. Lippman loves the music but wears dark glasses because she can't stand the lights!

Reared in Brooklyn, Sally worked as a stenographer in the advertising department of the old New York *Tribune*, finally went to law school, and in 1927, was admitted to the bar. She got married the same day. She didn't practice law, she said, because she found there was no justice. It is also possible, as she also says, that she didn't practice law because she didn't have to earn a living. Her husband did that.

Widowed three years ago, Mrs. Lippman now lives in a four-room co-op off Riverside Drive in Manhattan, and frequently entertains a wide assortment of guests at dinner parties that begin late—and usually end at Studio 54. Liza Minnelli has been a guest, and so have other show-biz types, journalists, publicists, and a handful of her young male friends, who are often taken for her grandsons.

"My psychiatrist said I was the grandmother figure," she says.

A dedicated golfer for years, she is now a dedicated disco dancer.

"I just love it," she told one interviewer. "I'll dance till the day I die."

And as much as Disco Sally loves dancing, that's how much the dancers, the press, and photographers love Sally who has become—at seventy-eight—something of a celebrity. Her brother may fear she is a laughing stock, but if anyone's laughing, it's Sally.

★★

Anthropologist Edward T. Hall, in *The Hidden Dimension*, a study of man's use of space in public and in private, shed some light on the phenomenon of large numbers of people dressing, dancing, and acting out their dreams and fantasies and enthusiasms on the disco dance floor:

"The great body of people today," he said, "feel a need to increase self-identity, to intensify experience, and to decrease alienation."

★★

En masque, anyone can be a star
1978 DISCOTHEKIN' NEWS/ DOCUMENT ARCHIVES

Roller-Arena is a familiar and popular figure on New York City's disco floors   DARLEEN RUBIN

Roller-Arena

One of the most colorful of the fantasy folk in New York City's discotheques is Roller-Arena, an apparition in a gossamer dress, wearing a flowered hat and carrying a wand, who dances the night away at Studio 54—on roller skates. During working hours, Roller (for short) is a hard-working, responsible young man. He started skating to work in 1970, when the threat of a subway strike gave him the idea. The strike never came off, but the skating did, and since then he has become a familiar figure, skating in street clothes or in what he calls "full regalia" on the streets, in Bloomingdale's, and in the discotheques.

One afternoon we sat in my living room and talked about how this phenomenon came into the disco scene:

"The first time I went to Studio 54," he said, "was on Hallowe'en night last year. I had heard all these things about how difficult it was to get in, and so forth . . . but when I arrived on Hallowe'en night and pulled up in a cab, a whole bunch of people began to applaud. . . . But I just got in line like everybody else and I waited five minutes and somebody came and took me in—and I've been going ever since.

"Sometimes, many times I've gotten up, got everything together, and skated down Park Avenue at two in the morning, then jumped in a cab at 79th and Park, gone over to Studio, and stayed till closing—and that I love! It's so—so New York!

"Full regalia—well, that is my turn-of-the-century ballgown, a hat that is Southern Baptist PTA, a wand. One magazine writer described me as a drag queen, which I am not. That's her terminology for a man who wears—well, I always say a ballgown or a Ginger Rogers chiffon fantasy. Personally, I like to say 'cross dresser.' I don't like the word drag queen or transvestite. It's a label. It puts you in a slot. . . .

"Some people don't understand. I think their upbringing has a lot to do with what they say—with what comes out of their mouth. Teenagers, for instance, are often—negative. I feel that a lot of young people who are still struggling for an identity may find a man or a woman, whatever, like me . . . whom they don't understand—they may react and retaliate negatively—verbally. But I know how to handle situations like that.

"After all—what I am wearing is only material things. You take that off, and there is a real person underneath. A lot of times I do a pirouette and just cut out."

Roller-Arena had brought along a large portfolio of press clippings, column "mentions," photographs: Roller-Arena skating down Fifth Avenue, Roller-Arena chatting with a group of police officers, Roller-Arena in the Easter Parade. . . .

"In the last year," he said thoughtfully, leafing through the pages, "I've begun to accept the fact that I am famous because of what I have created. One person the other day who is very much a part of the discotheque scene said that I was considered one of the most famous people in the New York City society disco scene today. Do you think this is true?

"Because—I mean, I think everybody makes things happen in this city, and besides, I think there are other things I've done besides roller skating that gives something to the city."

Like?

"Well—like just being nice to people perhaps."

Potassa

To the readers of the country's high-fashion magazines, Potassa is a familiar figure, a top model of women's clothes designed by some of the most famous designers in the country. Tall, shapely, dark-haired, and beautiful, Potassa has a wardrobe of some three hundred gowns, many of them gifts of designers who are glad to have their creations modeled.

On the floors of the city's discotheques, Potassa is also a familiar figure, dancing wildly with a partner, or elegantly solo, perhaps holding a red rose in full bloom. Sometimes carried away by the excitement of the evening—and the attention—Potassa does a strip on the disco floor. And those who hadn't known before, know then—that Potassa is a man.

"Well, I am a woman, every day, twenty-four hours a day, for years," says Potassa, who speaks with a strong Spanish

Whatever your fantasy, you can act it out at a disco
LE CLIQUE PHOTO

accent. "I'm more a woman than a man, because I was born, everything very feminine. Even with no makeup, a dress, a blouse, I look like a woman—I'm not really in drag—because, the trouble is I was born with something that says I am a man. But all my life, I have felt like a girl—a woman."

Potassa is a privileged member (non-paying) of Studio 54, where owner Steven Rubell feels she adds to the fantasy scene. Like anyone else, Potassa loves the VIP treatment. One time, "they grab me and bring me to come in right away without waiting, and they leave young John Kennedy still waiting outside!"

★★★

"In all my clubs, I like to watch the people on the dance floor," says Disco Queen Regine. "The way they move to the tempo of the music reveals their real selves. I can tell you who are the ones who have really come to dance—not just to be seen at Regine's.

"A good dancer always fascinates the crowd watching him. And each of his moves is like a sensual vibe of a good lover. Unfortunately, a good dancer is not always a good lover."

★★★

You've Got Magic

"Forty-nine *pipi* rooms—that is success!"

And *that* is Regine, the Frenchwoman with the pale white skin and brick-red hair whose name has become synonymous with elegance and chic and disco all over the world.

Her delight in the forty-nine elegant little stalls in the opulent ladies' room of her Paris "Regine's" was not a put-on. The lady—whose daytime appearance is one of a pleasant, plumpish housewife of good peasant stock—enjoys reminding her listeners—and perhaps herself—that she originally came "from the streets." That two-million-dollar Regine's on the rue de Ponthieu in Paris is a long way from the street stall where Regina (or Rachel) Zylberberg once peddled brassieres for a living . . . a long way from her father's café where she started working as a waitress at the age of thirteen.

Her lapses into vulgar street French, her nonchalant meanderings about elegant hotel halls clad only in a bath towel, her delight in going barefoot while shoes of all styles, colors, and price tags stand five layers deep on her closet floors—all these seem to heighten the pleasure of being Regine: Regine, the Queen of the Night; Regine, Doyenne of the Disco; Regine, to whom royalty bows and society scrapes.

Regine, who can sneeze in a public place and hear her good health wished in three languages at once.

This is the Regine of the silver-and-black plastic cards that magically open the doors of her clubs to some thousands upon thousands of the world's most Beautiful People. This is the businesswoman who knows that for seventeen hours out of every twenty-four, somewhere on three continents of the world, people are dancing in one or another of her elegantly beautiful clubs.

Headquarters for this empire of glamour, glitter, and gossip

Queen of the Night: Regine — GERARD BARNIER

is Regine's apartment above her club, New Jimmy's, in Paris. The lady, it is said, can work only if she is uncomfortable—sitting on the edge of the bed or perched on a rickety antique chair. She has proper business offices as well as apartments above all her clubs, but never appears in them, and she has been known to receive interviewing journalists while bathing in her black-plastic-snakeskin-lined bathroom.

The Regine apartment at the New York City operation is a bit less bizarre. While her staff deals with the telephones, the visitors, the mail, and the printers in offices down the hall, she receives friends and other visitors in her apartment on a high floor in the Delmonico Hotel on Park Avenue. In the late afternoon, the apartment—draped, carpeted, and upholstered in a sunny golden yellow—is flooded with sunshine and filled with arrangements of flowers. The glass-topped tables are a litter of press releases, photographs, teapots and cups, and the business and marketing letters on the distinctive pink stationery of Regine.

Regine works, thinks, drives, plans, and creates at a pitch of intensity that exhausts most of the people around her. She arrives in town like a tornado and departs the same way, leaving behind her a wake of exhausted staff and months of projects to be accomplished in weeks.

(Her gentle, darkly handsome young husband, Roger Choukroun, appears to be the only relaxed person in her entourage. To be with Regine, Roger gave up his job as a computer engineer, taking over the social duties of the family—and occasionally handling a minor business deal or two.)

Wherever she arrives, and wherever she works, her local staffs are tense with a mixture of anticipation, affection—and dread.

"When she is here," said one staffer, "it is go, go, go every minute. She wears us out. You never know when you will get home, and when you are home, you are afraid to pick up the phone. She is dynamic. This is her whole life. She does not seem to know this is not everybody's whole life."

In France, Regine is the bright red flame that attracts the international jet-set moths to her Paris clubs. In the United States, she draws all of New York's implausibly democratic mix—the fashion crowd, the theater bunch, and the society gang that likes nothing better than to dress up and go somewhere chic where there are sure to be photographers.

"At Regine's," says one discophile, "you don't go to dance—you go to see and be seen."

"At Regine's," added another, with just a hint of snobbery, "you can feel chic instead of old."

Old, chic, or just eager to be on display, princesses and princes, counts and movie stars, social climbers, beautiful young people, diplomats, the powerful, the political, and the merely rich find their nighttime home at Regine's. No matter in which country they may find themselves, at Regine's they feel they've never left home, for every Regine's is like every other Regine's—only more so.

There is the same elegant taste, the Art Deco figures with their stiff poses and egg-shaped faces . . . there is the lamé

. . . and the banquettes, the dark walls and mirrored ceilings, and the kindly light that smooths out wrinkles and miraculously erases bags and shadows.

Regine's New York was her first disco on the American continent, and last June her second opened, in Montreal, in the Hyatt Regency Hotel.

"People said I am crazy," she recalls with a slight smile. " 'For what are you going to do that?' they said. I said, 'For what not? In Montreal, you don't go out? You don't dance?' "

The Montreal disco, like her others, was designed by Alberto Pinto in her favorite Art Deco theme. New York's club was started for an estimated half-million dollars two years ago, boasting a then-extravagant $20,000 music system and a floor sculpture of four heart-shaped neon tubes that pulsate beneath the floor to the beat of the music.

Regine's discotheques are—by American standards—quite small. This enhances the feeling of crowding which is part of the pleasure of disco dancing, but it tends to discourage enthusiasm. The New York floor, in fact, is so small that on a

★★

Almost as soon as the disco doors slide back at a Regine's club, the DISCO FULL sign goes up. It is an old trick of Regine's, one she devised when she was just starting Chez Regine in Paris. (For this club on rue du Four, she chose a park theme; she decorated with trees she stole from the Bois de Boulogne and used park benches because she couldn't afford banquettes.)

For a month, the FULL sign on the door politely rebuffed all comers, while inside the music blared, and Regine sat with a handful of her friends—in an empty discotheque. When finally she did open the doors, she was besieged by a crowd gone mad with a month of gossip and rumors and guessing.

Is it a true story? Does the trick work?

"But, of course." Regine laughs. "Did they not do the same thing in New York when Studio 54 opened? It always works."

★★

Saturday night, the dancers are forced to move up and down like pistons in some colorful machine, since there is no room for them to move in any other direction.

"There are two ways of doing disco," says Regine. "A big place or a small one. My way is unique, to impose the personality of me. You cannot personaleeze two thousand people. But I like the big disco, too. Studio 54 is amusing. It is another—another walking."

Regine, who has been a successful disco entrepreneur for twenty-five years, is certain that the wave of dance fever will roll on for a long time.

"Today people like to escape troubles, to spend on themselves, not to put their money away for their children. The best thing in the United States is that everybody dances. In Europe, only the very young go to disco, but here, everybody dances, all ages.

"Some places will not stay forever. There is a great competition. It is a very difficult walking. After two years here, it is remarkable if a disco still exists. . . . But for me, it is a career, and not only for that. Look, I come from the streets . . . I like the glamour, the sophistication, the sexiness. . . ."

Regine already needs the fingers of two hands to count her successes—three clubs in Monte Carlo, two in Paris, one in Rio de Janeiro, in Bahia, in Trouville, Montreal, and New York.

And on the drawing boards are plans for a Regine's in Los Angeles, in Washington D.C., in London, Toronto, Caracas—and undoubtedly, many more.

That's a lot of *pipi* rooms.

Steve Rubell

"Guys try to hit me, girls try to kiss me. Girls who wouldn't say hello to me before are kissing me now. It's like all of a sudden, I'm so much taller, so much better looking."

Brooklyn-born Steve Rubell, thirty-four, is still only five-foot-four and weighs only 116 pounds, but within the past eighteen months, he has become a BIG MAN. Seven years ago, he was collecting unemployment checks at $75 a week.

Today, his estimated net worth runs between $1 million and $15 million.

This is the fast-talking, hard-working, hyped-up young man who is merely the co-owner and guiding genius of Studio 54, the biggest, the hottest, the most exciting, and most elaborate discotheque in the country. So far.

Dark-skinned, brown-eyed, and soft-spoken (most of the time), Rubell sometimes behaves like a pain-in-the-neck smart aleck overwhelmed by his sudden success. At other times, he is a diffident, eager kid in corduroy jeans and turtleneck sweater who likes nothing better than to run back and forth showing off his vast opera-house-turned-disco.

He clambers on railings at the balcony's edge to show off the best views, ushers guests into the deejay's booth where he fetches little green bottles of Perrier water to refresh them while they watch the magicians of light and sound at work.

Since April 26, 1977, his baby, the elegant, overwhelming Studio 54 on West 54th Street, near 8th Avenue in Manhattan, has become an internationally famous whirlpool of color, light, and sound that nightly sucks in celebrities, socialites, politicians, actors, promoters, diplomats, beautiful women, handsome men, and a spicy assortment of the freaky, the bizarre, and the just plain weird.

In the year of the disco phenomenon, Studio 54 has been the quintessence of the phenomenon—and Steve Rubell is the unlikely little guy who made it happen.

Sometimes he is suave and soothingly diplomatic in tuxedo and velvet tie. Sometimes, in jeans and jacket and scuffed sneakers, he seems completely out of place in his own place. Yet it is he, more often than not, who mans the entrance, surveying the glittering crowds behind the velvet ropes, deciding who does and who doesn't get in.

Not all his decisions are popular. One night, an angry customer knocked him down twice when Rubell refused him admission.

"I'll let anyone in who looks like they'll make things fun," says Rubell. "We like some guys with guys because it makes the dance floor hot, you know? There are certain people who come that we know are good."

Rubell has been known to point to a couple and declare to the girl, "You're pretty, you can come in," and then refuse to

Ian Schraeger and Steven Rubell, Studio 54's owners
TIM BOXER

let her escort in with her because he doesn't like his looks.

What he is after, says Rubell, is a good balance between straights and gays, men and women, blacks and whites, trendy and traditional. He lets some unemployed dancers and actors in free. But he discourages singles of either sex because he doesn't want the Studio to become a singles joint.

"I wouldn't let my best friend in if he looked like an East Side singles guy."

John Travolta, actor, might not have trouble getting into Studio 54, although one can never be sure. But "Tony Manero," the Brooklyn boy whom Travolta immortalized in *Saturday Night Fever*, wouldn't stand a chance.

"Would you let *you* in?" I once asked him. There was a pause and then a grin.

"Maybe—after six months or so."

Even the 3,700 cardholders—those who have a membership in Studio 54—aren't always sure they'll get in, a practice that has caused Rubell no little trouble and a few lawsuits.

The son of a former Brooklyn postal worker who worked as a tennis pro after leaving the post office at 4 P.M., Rubell himself became a ranked tennis player to please his father. But he always hated tennis, mainly, friends of the family say, because he hated competing with his older brother who was not only a better tennis player but was nearly a foot taller and a lot brainier than Steve.

(It's not unusual for Steve to introduce him as "my brother, the gynecologist. Doesn't he look smart? He's got an IQ of 170.")

Rubell didn't exactly start out as a boy wonder. He had attended Syracuse University, taking business courses which he said taught him nothing, and then, in 1971, he took his first job running a brokerage office on Wall Street. It paid $20,000 a year, but he didn't like it.

"I got no pleasure like you get out of dealing with people. I felt I was dealing with certificates." So he quit.

Late in 1971, he borrowed $13,000 from his parents (who really didn't care much for the idea of a restaurant business)

★★

Steven Rubell of New York's Studio 54 thinks disco has a "terrific future."

"People who had never been to discos before are going to discos now. And it's not just fashion people, and not just people with money—it's all kinds of people.

"After all, 98 percent of the people who come to Studio 54 are *not* celebrities."

★★

and opened a Steak Loft Restaurant in Rockville Centre, Long Island. By 1974, he had four of these family-type restaurants, and at one point, he even owned a discotheque called the Enchanted Garden, in Douglaston, Queens.

Noisy customers and disgruntled neighbors and legal complications later forced the disco to close, and Steve, who by then had already come down with disco fever, was looking for another location.

He found it in a huge building originally built as an opera house, which had opened in the first days of the Depression, quickly closed, served for a while as a federal theater, and finally became the CBS-TV studio where, among other shows, generations of TV viewers watched "What's My Line?"

"I wanted an old theater," says Rubell, "a place big enough for a circus, for a total environment . . . where all classes could mix in an exciting atmosphere . . . and that's what Studio 54 is all about."

The skeptics thought Rubell and his partners were crazy when they opened Studio 54 with a capital of $400,000—a third of which Rubell put up himself. His two partners are Ian Schraeger, a college friend and lawyer who takes care of financial and legal matters, and Jack Dushey, a discount retailer and very silent partner.

Before long, Studio 54 had become a gold mine, drawing between 1,000 and 1,500 people from Tuesday through Thursday, and more than 2,000 on Fridays and Saturdays—all at roughly $10 a head.

"If I never worked again, I'd never spend all the money I've made," says Rubell. "But it is difficult. You want people to like you for what you are."

Rubell lives in a $1,000-a-month apartment on the East Side, with three phones beside his bed in which he sleeps only about four hours a night—or a morning, from 6 A.M. after the Studio closes to 10 A.M. when he bounces out for a fast breakfast of Coca-Cola and Famous Amos chocolate chip cookies.

"It's like I can't sleep. I'm driven. I can't sit still."

Steve's parents (who still live in their $18,000 home in the Canarsie section of Brooklyn) are proud of their son's success although they don't quite understand it. They come into 54 once in a while but, says their son, "they're older, you know, and they don't really dig the scene. What they'd really like is for me to settle down and marry a nice girl and raise a family somewhere out on Long Island."

Right now, his parents' chances seem slim. Rubell had a ten-year relationship with a "wonderful girl" who finally one day said, "It's me or the business." Rubell's answer was: "The business." And now she's gone.

Rubell's business is the most important thing in the world to him these days and he's enjoying it.

"I love involving myself with people, in people's lives," he says, and these days those are people like Liza Minnelli, Mikhail Baryshnikov, designer Halston, Andy Warhol, Elizabeth Taylor, Truman Capote, Farrah Fawcett-Majors, Miz Lillian Carter, Bianca Jagger, Jackie Onassis's children—and on and on.

Now he is planning another Studio 54 in London, and perhaps one in Los Angeles, and maybe an entertainment park that would out-Disney Disney World. With bigger money and hungrier eyes now fixed on the booming disco scene, what will happen if someone builds an even more exciting, outrageous, and trendy discotheque, and Steve Rubell finds himself once more a short, skinny nobody?

"Then I'll do it all over again," he says simply. "If you did it once, you can do it again."

Maurice Brahms

One of the most experienced and most knowledgeable of today's disco entrepreneurs is also one of the most retiring, and the idea of being a disco king would fracture the usual calm of Brooklyn-born Maurice Brahms. A slender, aesthetic-looking man, Brahms's New York New York has been called by many in the field "one of the most beautiful discotheques in the world." More of a doer than a talker, Brahms was finally cornered in his office to talk about disco—past, present, and future.

Question: Why aren't you a celebrity entrepreneur like, say, Regine or Rubell?

Brahms: When you become a celebrity, you have to pay the price. Every move you make—every mistake you make—

becomes magnified. I'm more concerned with running a good, successful club and being known by the people who come into the club—the real disco people who really make the market—the ones who pay to go in.

Q: When did you get started in the disco field?

Brahms: About six or seven years ago, there were juice bars—no alcohol—and I noticed they were packing in large numbers of people to dance to records. And I thought if it could be done in a more professional manner, we could attract a lot of other people who wouldn't be caught dead in a juice bar with a jukebox.

Q: How did you start in the business?

Brahms: I had seen premises on Broadway, downtown, that were ideal for a disco, and I wanted something that would be entirely different. So I ventured into neon. People said I was crazy, that neon inside an enclosed space would drive people up a wall, drive them crazy. But I did it anyway, and it proved successful. That was Infinity—and it was the forerunner of popular clubs today.

Q: Where do you want to go in the future with disco?

Brahms: Well, New York New York is enough of a challenge at this moment. The restaurant and the cabaret theater portions of it will be finished this September, and then, if they are successful—as well as the disco—and running smoothly, I would be interested in doing something else.

(*Note:* Brahms is probably among the first to move in the direction of an entertainment place rather than simply disco alone. More and more people want a place to get away from the music, sometimes to relax and watch, sometimes for a place to eat. Such an entertainment place becomes like a private club, one place in which to do many things without having to hail a taxi or move the car.)

Q: What makes New York New York work?

Brahms: Well, it was conceived to be *not* a "disco" as the word "disco" goes, and not a "club"—like El Morocco—but as something that combined both. It has the elegance of El Morocco but not quite the up-tightness, plus the excitement of Infinity, but not quite the kookiness of *it*. New York New York appeals to segments of both kinds of disco-goers.

Q: What makes a club last, and how long can it last?

Brahms: In New York City, clubs have very short lives,

because New Yorkers are by far the most fickle, and are very avant-garde. New York New York (and others done well, on the same principle) should have a long life because it is not just a disco. I'd say about ten years.

Q: Do you play the door game at New York New York?

Brahms: We're a true membership club. Members are *guaranteed* admission. If the place is full, we have to refuse nonmembers. Otherwise, we welcome them. I think it is immoral to discriminate on the basis of people's appearance—their good looks, etc., but if it becomes a general policy in the field, I would have to go along.

Q: What are the risks that face anyone deciding to go into the disco business?

Brahms: The monetary risks in this business are astronomical. You only hear about the successful discos, but I would say that only about five of New York's best-known discotheques are really making money. The risks with people are great, too. People's temperaments and personalities can cause physical problems—people who are rejected—

Q: You mean, you could get punched!

Brahms: And then, it is a day-and-night business. The disco is open at night, but you have to be in the office in the daytime, to handle bookings and calls and other business matters. It is really a seven-day-a-week, twenty-four-hour-a-day business, and anyone who doesn't run it that way isn't going to make it.

Q: If you had a crystal ball, would you see a future for disco in it?

Brahms: Oh, yes. The rest of the country and the rest of the world will catch up to where New York is now—and that will go on for quite a number of years. But New York, I think, has reached a point where discos can't go on any longer as discos. They've got to become something more. Exactly what, I don't know. Maybe it'll be dancing in quicksand! I do know that people in New York are easily jaded. I don't think we can go on as we have been, which is one club opening after another, and knocking off the other club. I do think that discos will "peak." On the other hand, I think that dancing—and places to dance in—will be here for a long time.

Michael O'Harro

Michael O'Harro is young, brash, good-looking, and single. He is a self-proclaimed disco king, who, he says, created the singles' scene and singles' bar of the sixties, prophesied their demise, and helped to launch the disco phenomenon.

And he probably is—and did.

O'Harro, who is now trying to put together a trade association of discotheque owners, is the owner and operator of Tramps, one of the oldest and most successful discotheques in Washington, D. C. His projects and plans are dizzying—and may give an indication of which way disco is heading from here. A consultant ("for $500 a day, minimum two days") and author of a book, *How to Open a Discotheque*, he is putting discos into health spas—some thirty Holiday Health Spas on

Disco King Michael O'Harro himself

the East Coast, and is starting to license Tramps disco boutiques in department stores.

As a consultant, he says, he is unique because he doesn't "sell anything. I don't sell lighting systems or sound systems or anything else like that. What I sell is image, concept, marketing, public relations, and promotion."

Disco, he says, is not just a kind of sound—it's a place where someone plays records for dancing, and that means that while disco music may change, discotheques will remain. "There are country-western discos," he says, "rock-and-roll discos, golden-oldie discos. Disco has now come back, and it will be with us forever.

"For one thing, there's no question that we can't afford to go back to live entertainment. It's just too expensive."

O'Harro sees disco's future in the restaurant-disco concept.

"Every business that has a restaurant or entertainment facility will, if it is at all wise, be looking into the possibility of adding disco. This is the total entertainment concept—a total evening of dining and dancing, in one place."

O'Harro sees smaller discotheques as the most successful because they provide a feeling of intimacy, in an environment that turns customers into "stars."

"As discos spread to every city in America," he says, "you'll be able to know that you can get a good time anywhere, just by walking into a disco, because it will be like every other disco."

John Addison

John Addison, associate at New York New York, and owner of Boston/Boston and 15 Landsdown, both successful Boston discotheques, is known in the disco trade as the "father" of disco. He was the founder of Le Jardin, the premier discotheque of the sixties, which no longer exists except in the fond memories of dedicated discophiles.

A former waiter and juice bar owner, Addison—slim and faintly distant, wearing well-tailored suits—talks in a clipped British accent, and recalls with a satisfied smile that in 1965 he was turned down for a job at the famed Arthur disco run by

Sybil Burton Christopher, because he was "not the right type."

The door game, as it is played today at the trendy clubs like Studio 54, may have originated at Le Jardin. People were turned away there on grounds that had nothing to do with a customer's social class, race, or sexual preference but, rather, with the aura they projected in dress and personality.

At that time, Addison explains: "The people at Le Jardin were pretty, and with it. If someone was starchy-looking, they wouldn't add anything to the place. They'd be uncomfortable. There were a lot of stockbrokers I wouldn't let in."

These days Addison stays very much in the background of the disco scene and commutes between New York, Boston, the West Coast, and Europe.

Howard Stein

Howard Stein is not a disco king—yet, and the way things went for him on the opening night of Xenon, which was to be New York's newest trendy disco, he may never be. (Xenon opened prematurely, closed the next day, to reopen and try again.)

But Stein's is a familiar name to rock music lovers as a promoter of rock concerts—and they don't count him out too soon.

One of the country's most successful promoters, he was also one of the first to see the signs of creeping decay that overtook the rock concert scene. He was glad to get out.

"For years I lived surrounded by volume, aggression, back-stabbing, and quasi-violence in the streets and alleys of rock theaters around the country," he once said. "For a long time, I've felt a prisoner of one kind of environment and one kind of music."

The disco scene appears to suit the style of a man who makes a point of being seen in the best places at the right moments. He dresses in designer clothing and someone once commented that "he speaks Gucci" fluently. He has got about as far away as he could from his early years when he grew up on the Lower East Side across the street from what would become the Fillmore East, the rock cathedral of the sixties.

He trained as an actor at Carnegie Tech where, he says, he was the "golden boy of the drama department." But there wasn't enough money in theater to live on, and there followed a number of what he calls "embarrassing jobs," among them, one as an insurance agent.

"A whole generation of people are going to die and discover I mishandled their insurance papers. I had no idea of what I was doing."

There were some people who attended the opening night of Xenon who wondered the same thing. But when you've got the money to invest in a new venture, as Howard Stein has, you can afford to make mistakes—and correct them.

Van McCoy

"The Hustle" was written as an afterthought. Think about it.

The song that launched the current wave of dance fever in this country almost never got written. If a good friend and observant disc-jockey named David Todd hadn't nagged songwriter-arranger Van McCoy and his partner, Charlie Kipps, about a new "thing" that kids were doing on the floor of "Adam's Apple," a disco on New York's East Side, Americans might still be sitting around at night watching the Late-Late Show instead of getting out and creating their own great-great show in dance halls and discotheques all over the country.

Van McCoy, now thirty-four, and a lot richer man than he was back then in January, 1975, did not invent the dance. What he did was write the song. That was enough. With "The Hustle," McCoy did for the seventies what Chubby Checker had done for the sixties—set off a wave that swept people out of their seats and onto their dancing feet.

McCoy's song was a rendition in music of a dance beat that, up until then, was known only in a few Latin clubs in the South Bronx. It put "Hustle" into the vocabulary of everybody from Indianapolis to Tokyo, and helped move disco from popular pastime to a way of life for the seventies.

McCoy, a singer, arranger, and musician, had already actually completed the ten songs he needed for a new album of popular music he was putting together, and he was too busy working on arrangements to go look at that "thing" at Adam's Apple, so his partner went instead.

"It was very strange," said Kipps. "I stood in the disc jockey booth and looked down on the floor, and I noticed the steps were regimented and not random, and I thought, how did these kids choreograph themselves before they came to a disco?"

Shortly afterward, McCoy got one of the secretaries at his record company to show him the dance with a partner in the office and—almost as an afterthought—he wrote an eleventh song for the album, doing the melody and the arrangement at the same time. It was a catchy, bouncy number that fused Latin and rhythm-and-blues with a seductive vocal invitation to "do it, do the hustle." A record company executive, hearing it by accident, immediately labeled it *the* "single" to be promoted off the album. The rest is dance-and-music history.

The song gave national prominence to a smooth new set of steps that brought touch-dancing back to the dance floor. The album itself, renamed *Disco Baby* after "The Hustle" became a hit, sold eight million copies.

But McCoy didn't actually see the dance itself until he'd already written the song.

"I'd never seen anything like it since the jitterbug we did years ago," he said after watching a dance floor full of "hustling" young people. "It blew my mind."

McCoy attributes the overwhelming and unexpected success of The Hustle—both dance and song—to timing.

"People were getting tired of hearing how bad things were," he muses. "They needed to be reassured. I mean, how much negativity can you give people before they will seek escape in a positive direction? Maybe, before, there was no need for discos. But people now need to communicate more than they have for the last ten years. I think this is why they are seeking more communication on the dance floor."

McCoy's life has been devoted to music since he was old enough to see over a keyboard, which was at the age of four. The son of an engineer, McCoy was born in Washington, D.C., January 6, 1944, and was given piano lessons at the age of four by his mother, who played piano in church and wanted him to have an early musical foundation. His older brother, Norman, had studied violin from the moment he was old enough to hold the instrument, and soon Van and Norman began singing at church socials as the McCoy Brothers, and appeared at every ladies' tea around Washington.

"They passed the plate," McCoy remembers. "Sometimes we went home with fifteen bucks. I was eight. I thought I was set for life."

Nevertheless, McCoy gave up his performing career but continued his interest in music and, at the age of twelve, wrote his first song. As a teenager, he and his brother and three high school buddies formed what he calls a "doo-wop" group, and later, for a while, he sang with Mitch Miller's group.

McCoy had been in the music industry fourteen years before "The Hustle" broke, and he was doing a lot of writing for—and producing of—other groups such as Gladys Knight and the Pips, the Shirelles, and Peaches and Herb. But it was "The Hustle" that established him as a recording star in his own right. *The New York Times* called "The Hustle" "the biggest dance record of the seventies, and the biggest disc of that genre in nine years." It went to Number One on all the record charts all over the world, and by the end of 1975, McCoy had made an unprecedented sweep of the music trade magazine polls as "Top Instrumental Artist."

He received a Grammy Award when "The Hustle" was chosen Best Pop Instrumental by the National Academy of Recording Arts and Sciences. Not long afterward, his home town, Washington, D. C., proclaimed a Van McCoy Day, and his achievements were read into the *Congressional Record*. He received a gold album for *Disco Baby*, and offers for movie soundtracks, TV theme songs, and commercials poured in.

"I wasn't ready for the success of the song in the slightest," McCoy says now. "It happened too damn fast. I didn't even have a business manager at the time. I didn't get many personal appearances, all the things you're supposed to do when you get a hit."

After its initial impact, "The Hustle" died down. McCoy went on producing, but his follow-up records played on the same Hustle theme, and went nowhere.

"Maybe I went along with the same gag a little too much," he admits now.

"People thought of me as the Disco Kid. . . . Now I'm ready for the limelight. I feel I missed out on the exposure the last time because it took me so much by surprise, left me too little time to shift the focus of my thinking. Now, I'm on top of everything."

In the fall of 1977, McCoy moved into performing. He put aside the hard-driving Hustle beat, wrote songs for a new album that reflect the more mellow disco sound that is around now. The album, released in March of 1978, is *Van Allen McCoy*, and it touches on a wide variety of musical styles. One reviewer said he seemed to be "paying his respects to every kind of music."

The royalties from "The Hustle" and his long career have made Van McCoy a wealthy man. He owns three homes, two in Washington, D. C., and one—a $250,000 English Tudor mansion—in Englewood, New Jersey, where he moved in 1976 to be closer to his partner and to business in New York. Here he works and plans his career as a performer, writer, and musician.

"Look," he said, "let's be honest. Everyone has a vehicle. The Hustle was my vehicle. Whatever I do for the rest of my life was made possible by the Hustle, and now it's time to move on to other things."

The Bee Gees

When Robert Stigwood, the Australian impresario and genuis behind *Saturday Night Fever*, first asked the Bee Gees to write the theme song for that now-historic film, his instructions—according to Barry Gibb—were:

"Give me eight minutes—eight minutes and three moods. I want frenzy at the beginning. Then I want some passion. And then I want some w-i-i-i-l-d frenzy!"

When the Brothers Gibb finally sat down in Paris to write the title song for the film, the one they came up with was "Stayin' Alive," and it fairly drooled with frenzy and fiery excitement. In the pace and the lyrics of "Stayin' Alive" were all the passion and the yearning for personal freedom and escape that John Travolta expressed so convincingly in his portrayal of Tony Manero, a Brooklyn boy finding his way to manhood and identity in a neighborhood discotheque.

Later, along with Albhy Galuten and Karl Richardson, the Bee Gees wrote and co-produced the majority of the *Saturday Night Fever* soundtrack album. It contained many new Bee Gees songs and many old ones, as well as music of other groups, and it produced a dance fever that is still raging across the country. Within less than six months of its release in November, 1977, *Saturday Night Fever* had erased all previous record-holders as the biggest grossing album in the history of the recording industry.

By the time the Brothers Gibb are through harvesting the crop of that soundtrack, it is estimated they will have sold more than 12 million albums—and that's a double disc that has retailed at nearly $13. Even figuring discounts, the money "crop," it is conservatively estimated, will come close to the $120-million mark—a sum that will enable the Brothers Gibb to engage in something just a little bit more than staying alive.

Yet, just four years ago, the Bee Gees seemed passé, spent, washed-up—absolutely finished.

"We couldn't have sold ice cubes in the Sahara," says Robin Gibb.

Robin, twenty-nine, and his nonidentical twin, Maurice, and older brother Barry, thirty-one, form the nucleus of the Brothers Gibb. The boys have been performing professionally together since they were kids, when their father, Hugh, a bandleader, took his family from Manchester, England, to Brisbane, Australia, to escape the grim years of postwar England of the fifties.

Coached by their father, the brothers first started singing at the speedway stadiums in Australia. In 1958, Barry, Maurice, and Robin were christened The Bee Gees—and were on their way to eventual international renown. Barry was eleven. The twins were nine.

Impressed by their vocal harmonies, the speedway organizer introduced them to top Australian deejay Bill Gates; and Gates, in turn, started to play Bee Gees tapes on his radio show. Before long, the boys had their own half-hour TV show.

The Brothers Gibb: The Bee Gees found a new career in the disco sound   WIDE WORLD PHOTOS

They made their first big move in 1962 when they signed with one of Australia's major record labels. But it wasn't until 1967 when they and the rest of the family went back to England that they hit it big. A single called "Spicks and Specks" became a number one hit in Australia after the family had reached England.

Within their first week in London, they met Robert Stigwood, who was impressed. "I loved their composing," he recalls. "I also loved their harmony singing."

"Spicks and Specks" had brought them acclaim in Australia; and in the following spring, their first single in England—"New York Mining Disaster"—brought them their first hit in both England and in the United States. From then on—and throughout the remainder of the sixties—the Bee Gees were Biggies—scoring hit after hit.

Then suddenly, they went cold. They came down with a fever of their own—the ego fever that followed two years of international fame and glory. Robin bolted the group in 1969 to put out a solo that went nowhere. Maurice and Barry produced a television special they now confess was "terrible."

And all the while they shunned one another personally, they used the technique of vocal "overdubbing" to make their solo efforts sound like the familiar multipart harmony that had made them so successful. But nothing worked any more.

"We were nearly in oblivion by the time we realized we were in trouble," they recall.

After a year of frustration, the boys reassembled.

"We had to get back together because the formula was among the three of us," says Maurice. "But the image of the Bee Gee brothers had been smashed. We knew it would take five years to get to know each other again like we did before we started arguing."

It didn't take five years, but it did take nearly three. There were songs and singles and even some hits, but they still didn't really have a formula. Then they decided to retain Atlantic Records' Arif Mardin, a rhythm and blues specialist known as the "doctor of music." Mardin challenged the group to try a contemporary sound for the first time. Their forte had always been ballads, but in the dawning age of disco, ballads no longer sold. What saved them was a fresh disco slant.

"We were always capable of writing that kind of music," says Barry, "but we were too scared to have the confidence that we could play it as good or better than others. I think the main lesson we learned was that the music has to be vibrant. It has to have some magic about it."

"We're writers," says Robin, "and when you've got that gift, the ability to create a hook, the catch that makes people hum, you never lose it. You might go down the wrong road temporarily. But sooner or later you straighten up, you see what you've been doing wrong. Then it all comes flooding back."

It certainly has come flooding back. Since November, 1977, the "catch that makes people hum" has been in evidence from coast to coast. According to the music experts, the formula for the Brothers Gibb's new and phenomenally successful music style is something like this.

It blends two styles—one, the urgency of disco, and the

other, a middle-of-the-road romanticism. Put together, they produce a fresh-sounding mix of kinetic moving bassline and a whining, insistent, floating, soothing high male harmonizing.

Barry, thirty-one, is the group's guitarist and most prolific songwriter. Maurice is the bassist and the group comedian. Robin does not play an instrument on stage, but his and Maurice's tenors serve as an elegant frame for Barry's gutsy baritone.

It all adds up to a rich feast for the ears. And the chances are that now that they have found the combination, the sound will go on for a long time.

"The Bee Gees aren't a band that will do disco for the rest of their lives," says the boys. "If this stops working, we'll go on trying other kinds of music. Our music will always go on. We might get too old one day to *sing* it, but until then, we don't intend to stop."

The Bee Gees are affable people, easy to talk to, easy to get along with, totally without pretension. With their families, they are ensconced in their new home in Miami, Florida, writing their music, drinking their tea, dropping in once in a while at the local discotheques.

"People these days don't want to hear about how bad times are," says Barry. "I think they are far more interested in dancing and enjoying themselves now. The important thing in life is you're supposed to have a ball."

The Bee Gees, it would seem, are having a ball.

"It's a living," says Maurice Gibb, then adds with a grin. "Anyway, it beats work."

★★

As founding members of "Music for UNICEF," the Bee Gees have promised to turn over every dollar they make from a song they will record as part of the "Year of the Child, 1979."

Announcing this generosity, UNICEF'S executive director, Henry R. Labouisse, referred to the group as "The Beatles." The audience gasped, but nobody said anything. The Bee Gees said they'd give the money anyway.

★★

Jean-Marc Cerrone

Cerrone, the twenty-six-year-old French disco artist, has hit all the top charts since he started doing his own thing two years ago, and has sold more than 8 million copies of his three albums since he went from producing, writing, and playing for other people, to doing the same thing for himself.

Cerrone, Cerrone's Paradise, and *Cerrone 3—Supernature* have kept dancers moving and cash registers ringing since 1976. Billboard's Disco Forum IV, for 1978, named him the Disco Artist of the Year, Male Disco Artist of the Year, Disco Composer of the Year, Best Producer of a Disco Record, Disco Music Arranger of the Year, and Disco Instrumentalist of the year.

There is hardly a less likely candidate for this kind of success than Jean-Marc Cerrone, the youngest of three children of a small shoe manufacturer. Cerrone, who speaks only French, talks through an interpreter:

"I was always being kept after school because I used to snap on my desk with a ruler to the music I imagined. At home, it was the same thing, except with forks on the dinner table. Finally, for my birthday, my father bought me a small drum; then a second one; a bigger set, and so on."

Cerrone was making music when he was twelve, and working with groups by the time he was fourteen. At eighteen, after getting his diploma as a hairdresser, he decided he'd rather be a musician.

In September, 1976, he went to London's famed Trident Studios to produce "Love in C Minor," and when the French record companies passed it up, he went back to England and turned it out himself. Then he sold the albums himself, and promoted them in all the French discos. Atlantic Records' custom label, Cotillion, issued "Love, etc." in February, 1977, and it became a fixture in the Top 3 slot of the Record World and Billboard disco charts for two months. It also made the Top 30 ranks of rhythm and blues best-seller charts at the same time.

Cerrone, top disco performer of the year ATLANTIC RECORDS

But Cerrone already had *Cerrone's Paradise* in the works, and that one took Europe by storm.

The French press said: "Disco is easy, but disco Cerrone-style—only one person can do it."

His last album, *Cerrone 3—Supernature*, took fourteen months to produce and is a break from the rigid disco format.

"It's a story of good and evil," says Cerrone. "What I want to say to people is to leave each thing in its proper place, otherwise the monsters will be coming. Actually, the monsters exist within ourselves. . . .

"Frankly, I'm afraid I might lose a certain public (one side of the record is not disco) but sometimes you have to say 'to hell with the consequences.' If you want to do something—do it."

Donna Summer, Top Lady of Disco, started singing in church
WIDE WORLD PHOTOS

Donna Summer

Her first hit record was banned by the BBC, burned by an irate evangelist preacher in Tallahassee, Florida, and was known as "that record you turn off when the kids are listening." But for Donna Summer, that panting perpetration of "Love to Love You, Baby" opened the door to a music-singing-acting-nightclub career that has already made her rich, famous, and securely ensconced as the First Lady of Disco. And she is just getting started.

"Love to Love You, Baby" was recorded as a good-natured takeoff on some of the sex-soaked numbers that were making the charts in Europe several years ago. It caught the ear of Neil Bogart, the guiding genius of Casablanca Records, who sensed immediately that it could be a big hit—if it got plenty of what he called "bedroom play."

"I told the guys all I wanted for them to do was get the record played once, on one station, at midnight. If they did, I knew we'd sell records. The next thing I know, New York is going crazy."

Now that she has put a couple of years and plenty of professional distance between herself and that record, Summer can be philosophical. "Well, you have to get people's attention some kind of way," she says. "But I'm not just sex, sex, sex."

She was in those days, though, for "Love, etc . . ." was remarkable in a number of ways. The lyrics (which she wrote) consisted almost entirely of the five words of the title, repeated twenty-eight times, and interspersed with groans and grunts and languishing moans, erotic yelps, and a symphony of thumping guitars.

The album "for people to take home and fantasize in their minds" ran sixteen minutes and fifty seconds, and broke all rules of radio programming. Within weeks, Donna Summer was dubbed the Queen of Sex Rock and the First Lady of Love.

It was a singular accomplishment for a young woman who had started her singing career in church.

Donna Gaines Summer grew up in Boston in a loving but competitive family of five sisters and a brother. Her father, Ernest, a butcher, was so strict about his daughters that he would not permit them to wear lipstick or nail polish. Her mother, now a schoolteacher, then worked in a sneaker factory. At home and at school, Donna remembers that all the kids had to fight to find, and maintain, their own identities—and she found hers in music.

Her first musical inspiration, she says, was the gospel singing of Mahalia Jackson. Then, one Sunday, when the soloist at the Grant AME Church became ill, Donna, age ten, filled in for her.

"I found I was singing, not whispering or screeching; and suddenly my father was crying and the rest of the congregation was crying along with him. I had touched all of them. In that moment, I became a human being."

She also became a compulsive gospel singer. Donna spent every Sunday in the Grant AME Church, and attended as many as four or five other churches each Sunday, singing solos or with gospel groups.

Later on, she hooked up with some white rock musicians in the Boston area, listened to a lot of Janis Joplin and the Velvet Underground, and planned a singing career. But she wanted to be an actress, too. In New York, she auditioned for a role in *Hair* as a replacement for Melba Moore. Instead, she was offered the starring role in a European company of the show, and she took it. The show took her to Germany.

There she met and married blond Helmut Sommer who was also in the cast of *Hair*. She anglicized her husband's name and became Donna Summer. She and Helmut, now separated, "had some very good days together," Donna says, but "we came from very different backgrounds and we never really got to know each other well enough to stay together. But we are still good friends."

Their daughter, Mimi, now five, is a light-skinned, pretty child who lives most of the time with Donna's parents. Donna wishes the marriage had worked out, she says, because "a child really needs both parents." Because she travels a lot, she leaves the little girl in the care of the child's grandparents in Boston.

But when her mother is "at home" in her rented palazzo in

Beverly Hills, Mimi is with her, chattering away in both English and German, and slipping off with Donna to a hill behind the house when too many people and publicists and photographers move in.

"Having Mimi changed my whole life," Donna says. "As soon as she was born I realized that Wow! suddenly someone else has become a real part of your life. . . . She may be in one part of the world and I'm working in another, but she will always know I'm *there*."

Donna had already been a rising star in Europe, long before "Love to Love You" had made the trip across the Atlantic and made her a household—or, at least, a boudoir—word in this country. She had not only starred in the Munich company of *Hair*, she also modeled, did studio sessions, and sang in light opera. Producers Giorgio Moroder and Pete Bellotte had heard her sing, signed her up—and soon, one Donna Summer record hit after another was hitting the European continent.

Donna's *Once Upon a Time* was an ambitious two-record set that dominated the disco floors throughout the winter and spring of 1977-78. "Anything Donna Summer sings, people will dance to," one discophile said. The story in this record tells of a young woman's search for identity, and the singer not only co-wrote all the lyrics but also developed the concept with her co-managers.

The album's songs range from catchy, upbeat rock numbers to poignant ballads, and have finally convinced the critics that Donna Summer can do something more than heavy breathing.

"I know the industry refused to consider me a legitimate singer," she says. "But it just made me work harder. A lot of people run from obstacles. I say, let's show 'em. I don't compete with other people. I only compete with myself. I want to see if I can go one more step."

Thank God It's Friday, one of the first of the rising flood of disco movies to follow on the success of *Saturday Night Fever*, was one more step for Summer, who emerged, one critic said, as "both the Diana Ross and the Bette Midler of disco." But that was last season's accomplishment. Donna now has other projects in mind.

She wants to make a lot of money—not, she swears, to be able to move into a more lavish house or trade in her leased Mercedes for a Rolls Royce. Her dream is to build a commune—one with houses, schools, a clinic—everything, for poor black children in Brazil. She already has made sketches for the buildings.

Summer helps design the covers of her albums and is an inventor and something of an interior decorator as well. That commune, if it ever materializes, will undoubtedly be one of the most chic nonprofit institutions on the scene. In the meantime, however, nightclub acts, concert tours, more record albums, and more acting are on her busy agenda.

"I always wanted to be an actress, but there were no black roles when I got started," she says. "Musical theater was the only compromise I could find. I'll always record, but it might become secondary to me. I don't want to be known for just one thing."

"That's what I'm trying to say in the album, in 'Once Upon a Time,' that it's possible for people to do what they want to do. 'Fairy Tale High' is my favorite song in the album. It's believing that things are possible."

Grace Jones

She roars up the ramp onto the stage on a motorcycle, dressed in a skimpy animal skin or a slash of fabric that leaves a brown breast bare, a bronze leg naked to the waist, seizes the microphone as if it were a mace, and begins to snarl her biggest disco hits. Arrogant and arresting, she flings the lyrics into the faces of her adoring audience who howl and clap and leap and stomp and love every outrageous minute.

She is Grace Jones, twenty-five, a former dancer, former high-fashion model, occasional movie actress. Now a singer with what she describes as a "not too anything" voice, she has become, within a matter of months and one smash record, the current queen of the discos.

Wherever she appears, she packs her admirers in and creates pandemonium. The epitome of the disco seventies, Jones is one part talent, one part drive, and one part pure hype, for Grace is a prime natural resource for writers, gossip columnists, and photographers.

She looks about six feet tall, but insists she's three or four

Grace Jones, Queen of Pandemonium — FRANCIS ING

inches shorter. Her legs are long, her body slender and muscular, and her hair is either close-cropped or shaved off altogether. She has what have been described as "reptilian" eyes, high cheekbones, and long white teeth. She doesn't "wear" clothes, she says. They "assemble themselves" on her.

A typical "assembly" would include high-heeled shoes, dancers' knitted leg warmers, off-the-shoulder blouse, and a chinstrap cap. People stare at her on the street and she stares back and sometimes sticks out her tongue. It's one of the perquisites of being a disco queen.

Actually, Grace had been an underground, uncrowned "queen" for years before the square world discovered her, the darling of the gay disco crowd, haunting New York City's day world of dance studios, photo studios, salons, fashion shows, and openings, and the night world of polysex baths, private clubs, and discotheques.

In the days when Le Jardin was *the* disco that ruled Manhattan, Grace Jones was its acknowledged queen. Night after night, she ruled the dance floor like the John Travolta character in *Saturday Night Fever*, moving, dancing, creating. And every move she made, every step she took, was watched, and studied, and copied a hundred times over.

And like the Travolta character, the sheer force of her obsession with music and movement and her feverish drive for self-expression dominated the room and everyone in it. Today she dominates the room and everyone in it from coast to disco coast, from behind a microphone on stage, or from a spinning vinyl platter where her voice is amplified and magnified and pushed through costly and complicated sound systems that brainwash the dancers by sheer volume and intensity.

The person behind the personality was born on the island of Jamaica into a family of established politicians and preachers. Her grand-uncle had been a bishop; her father was a preacher who left the island for America while Grace was still a baby. She and her twin brother grew up loved and protected, and yet outsiders, in a mélange of aunts and uncles and siblings and cousins. It was a lonely experience.

"We lived like stray mongrels, scavenging and roaming," she says, "taking what we needed, then sneaking off and hiding all on our own."

When the twins were teenagers, they moved to America, joining their father who was then preaching in Syracuse, New York. And Grace, who had grown up virtually a wild child, free to do as she pleased, found herself in a middle-class world of shopping centers and drive-ins, of schools and rules.

"I never understood the rules," she says. "I can't behave. I don't know how."

She fought the system. She rebelled. She cursed. She wore Afros before they became fashionable, and she displayed her breasts long before nudity was acceptable undress. The local folk regarded her as a crazy girl. Her report card described her as "socially sick."

College couldn't hold her long, and Grace ran off to Philadelphia where she studied in drama workshops and sang in soul groups. Then she ran off to New York. And then she ran off to Europe, to Japan, to Hollywood, to South America, to Canada.

In great demand as a model, her face appeared in *Vogue* (both French and U.S. versions), in *Elle*, in *Pravda*. She has promoted beaver in Canada and has lent her face to the labels on cans of axle grease.

Returning to New York, she found that modeling no longer satisfied her, and since singing had always been one of her primary obsessions, she decided on a career in music. She acquired a manager and a press agent; and Tom Moulton, the acknowledged "master of the disco mix," was hired as her producer. In the summer of '77, Island Records released her first effort—a single called "I Need a Man." The music was so-so, the lyrics were nothing, but the rhythm and the beat

★★

Grace Jones sings against a special "tracking" tape when she makes her personal appearances. She makes the tapes in advance—with everything but the vocals on them—and then actually sings against the tape as she performs.

"It's difficult to sing over a tape," she says, "but I do it this way because it's better for discotheques."

★★

could knock you down, and the title line was repeated with such insistence and hunger that after a night of dancing for hours to other tunes as well, that's the one dancers went home humming.

"I Need a Man," and later the disco version of "La Vie en Rose," have made Grace Jones a star, a personage. Her antics have become news. When she arrives for a live performance, powering up the ramp on a motorcycle, escorted by bare-to-the-waist body-beautiful types, and cracking a whip like a lion tamer, her fans go wild.

Appearing in New Dimensions, a gay disco in Cleveland, she arrived an hour and fifteen minutes late, rode up the ramp accompanied by three male dancers, and sang her numbers to a "backing tape"—a tape with all of the music to which she sings the vocal. She walked through the crowd, said one reviewer, as only she could walk through a crowd, and languished across the piano for "What I Did for Love" and changed costumes on stage behind a cloud created by a fog machine.

In June, 1978, a new Manhattan discotheque launched its opening with a birthday party for Grace Jones. The main attraction, aside from Grace herself, was an eight-foot-high birthday cake garnished with 2,000 carnations and crowned by an honest-to-roaring gold Honda motorcycle. Two handsome, muscular young men clad only in black silk jockstraps guarded the cake for hour after chilly hour in the air-conditioned disco. ("Well, you have to start somewhere," said the one nearest me, with a shrug and a grin.) Upstairs, guests gorged themselves on fruits and vegetables and dips and pastries arranged on long tables on which the centerpieces were half-clad, good-looking boys, wearing white shorts and arrangements of bananas, cherries, apples, and other assorted goodies.

It was all very "Grace Jones-ish," and when the lady herself arrived, there was the usual crush to get near as she climbed aboard the Honda, allowed those long legs to be caressed by the handsome young guards, and fluttered her golden eyelids and made reptilian eyes at the photographers who seemed to outnumber the guests. It was a scene fit for a disco queen. For the moment.

"The way it goes with me is, every scene becomes a prison," she once confessed. "The moment that I'm balanced and anything gets routine, I feel trapped. Wherever I went, whatever I did, I wanted the same thing, the one thing I've always yearned for, ever since I can remember."

And what was that?

"More."

Gloria Gaynor

Gloria Gaynor was officially crowned the Queen of Disco in 1975 by no less a personage than then-Mayor Abraham Beame of New York City. It was her "Never Can Say Goodbye," a fifteen-minute-long, played-at-one-clip-for-dancing record that helped kick off the disco music craze, and it is considered a watermark record in the music field.

Queen Gloria is also credited with being the primary force behind the influence of female vocalists in today's disco sound.

A middle child, surrounded by five brothers and a sister, Gloria was born and raised in Newark, New Jersey, and her interest in music began when she was growing up. In this, she was encouraged by the whole family, including her brothers whose voices, she says, were even better than hers.

"They could even harmonize with the water pipes!"

At the age of eight, Gloria turned on to rock-and-roll, but by the time she was thirteen, she was really serious about singing, and she "studied" with the recordings of every artist she admired. She learned diction from Nat King Cole, styling from Sarah Vaughan. Then, at eighteen, she had a chance to sing with a group that had lost its vocalist. She quit her job as an accountant, told everybody she was going to be a big star, and went off to sing with the band. The gig lasted three weeks—and that was it for the next three years.

One night, in Newark, Gloria visited a club with a friend who—behind her back—convinced the band to call her to the mike. They hired her that night. From then on, she worked steadily, six shows a night, six nights a week, with only two weeks off in two years. Then one day she went into a studio to record "Never Say Goodbye," and the rest is disco history.

In the years since then, Ms. Gaynor has been trying to break out of—although not away from—the disco pigeonhole.

Gloria Gaynor, Polydor Records' disco queen
COURTESY OF POLYDOR INCORPORATED

She doesn't want to be regarded strictly as a disco singer, "but rather as a good singer with the ability to show depth and variety."

Nevertheless, her most recent album, *Gloria Gaynor: Park Avenue Sound*, for Polydor Records, has been hailed as "the ultimate disco."

Being royalty, even a disco queen, can be an educational experience, Gloria says.

"It's let me know—and made me want to let everybody else know—that the only difference between people anywhere is culture. The differences are only differences; and they do not make you any better or worse.

"Sometimes the differences are really beautiful."

Let's All Chant

The music at a disco never stops—not for a breath, not for a moment. From the second that tribal beat begins to move through the tweeters and woofers and boom boxes and all the other electronic gadgets that make up a discotheque's highly sophisticated sound system, it does not stop until the last dancer has boogied out the door into the dawn's early light.

The volume ranges from very loud to overwhelming, and in some places, it can make your eardrums hurt and your rib cage vibrate.

Disco music has been described by critics as "the ultimate in plastic," "overproduced," with lyrics that are "pointless" at best, "tasteless" at worst. It *is* lush, much more so than soul music, and much sweeter and easier to take than rock. Born in New York out of a combination of black and Latin music (the famed "Philadelphia sound" that helped spawn disco is "black" sound), disco music weaves together the varicolored strands of rhythm and blues, Motown and soul. The end product combines a number of music styles from different eras: the dance music of the twenties, Big Band effects of the forties, lush string arrangements, and choruses or vocalists singing lyrics which, to the untrained ear, are usually unintelligible.

And at the heart of it all is the disco beat—an up-tempo, heavy, straight four-four time that goes directly to the feet and guides them like a metronome.

It is automated, pure music without any messages or hidden meanings. It is also, in the sensual environment of the discotheque, hypnotic and compelling, erasing thought and turning dancers into wind-up disco dolls on a joyful trip to a mindless, sweaty good time.

Which is what disco as a phenomenon is all about. The purpose of disco is not just simply music, it is dance.

"It's the American Graffiti of the eighties," says Issy Sanchez, director of disco promotion for Atlantic Records. "Disco happened because people wanted to dance and wanted entertainment."

Although there is only one purely disco label, Salsoul Records, not quite three years old (three out of every five of its records are disco), most pop music companies are including disco music in their yearly output. For executives and bookkeepers in the record business, looking at that famous bottom line, the magic word is "crossover." Says Kenn Friedman, Salsoul's promotions' director: "The crossover is the goal of every recording company."

Ray Caviano of TK Records (which turns out about 50 percent disco music) agrees. Much of his company's energies and sales, he says, are dedicated to parlaying a song that has been recorded as disco into a song that crosses out of the disco category into rhythm-and-blues programming on radio, and the Top 100 of the popular music charts.

The crossover is the jackpot of the disco gamble.

That is when you begin to hear disco on radio, for very few stations actually program all-disco music. A hit disco number can sell as many as 200,000 records before it is ever heard on radio. It is the disco deejays, not the radio disc jockeys, who "break" disco records.

"When a new record comes into a radio station, it must wait its turn before it's picked from a bin," explains Phil Gill, Polydor Records promotions director. "By that time, the people who go to discotheques are tired of it, because they've been hearing it at the clubs already."

But the rest of us are also hearing more and more of the disco sound. You hear it on TV sports broadcasts and at all the big sports stadiums across the country. Increasingly, it's the music behind the commercial and the beat that heightens suspense and excitement on TV dramas.

"The mass appeal acceptance of disco is just now happening," says Ray Caviano of TK Records. "Disco is a social revolution. That's why disco music is constantly changing. It's a people movement."

Disco—the sound, the place, the music—are what's happening in the popular culture today. These are some of the people who are making it happen.

Linda Clifford, runaway hit   WARNER BROTHERS RECORDS

Linda Clifford

If Linda Clifford's friends could see her now, they'd flip. A former Miss New York State, she has been singing and recording for a number of years, but much of the time she seemed to be associated with small record companies that folded right after she signed. Then she signed with Curtom Records.

Her first album, *Linda*, included "From Now On," which became a disco smash and a radio hit in the fall of 1977. Her second time out, *"If My Friends Could See Me Now,"* was top-of-the-charts in discotheques for months in the 1978 disco season.

In the *Friends* album, Linda teamed with Gil Askey, a former Motown producer, and with Curtis Mayfield stepping in to help produce a couple of selections. Standouts on the record are Askey's "Runaway Love," another disco hit—and an energetic number that dancers have been responding to enthusiastically.

A former Brooklynite, Linda was pleased with the success of her records—especially when her first record played New York.

"In New York, they played 'From Now On' twice an hour on all the major stations," she says, "and since my whole family lives in New York, my phone was ringing all the time with relatives saying 'We *heard* you!' It was really nice."

At *Billboard* magazine's Disco Forum, 1978, Linda was named Most Promising New Disco-Artist of the year.

The Village People

In case you hadn't noticed, that exuberant bunch of vocalists who call themselves the Village People are a gang of fantasizers. One look at the cover of their *Macho Man* Casablanca album that's been knocking them dead on disco floors this season will clue you that these guys represent just about every fantasy going, from cowboys and Indians to Easy Rider.

There is Randy Jones, the Cowboy in Stetson and leather chaps;

David "Scar" Hodo, the Construction Worker, in hard hat;

Felipe Rose, the Indian, in full feather;

Glenn Hughes, the Leatherman, in full leather, plus shades and a hairy chest;

Alexander Briley, sometimes called Soldier;

Victor Willis, the shined-up Superstar in glittering shirt and black boots, "Officer of Love," who is the lead vocalist and lyricist.

An equally important member of the group doesn't open his mouth—not in front of the microphones, anyway. He is Jacques Morali, a Frenchman who brought the group together in 1977 and who writes most of the music, with the collaboration of Victor Willis.

Village People—which includes six men in the band as well as the six vocalists—has been dubbed by Dick Clark as "the most exciting group since the 1950s."

Dave Hodo, the Construction Worker, says they're like "the cast from a Broadway show or a movie."

The VPs are not just another bunch of pretty faces, either. They have other talents, both as a group and as individuals.

Victor Willis starred in several Broadway musicals, including *The Wiz*, and Randy Jones got his experience in TV plays and dance theater. Glenn Hughes previously staged his own one-man dramas, while David Hodo recalls how he once wore roller skates and ate fire simultaneously on "What's My Line." Felipe Rose is an innovative professional dancer, and Alexander Briley is a brilliant vocalist.

The People, says Hodo, see themselves as a People's Liberation Group, selling a kind of do-your-own-thing philosophy and expressing the fantasies of every boy and girl—as well as trying to convey a very positive male, if not macho, image.

In their first year, their debut album *Village People* won them recognition from *Billboard*, *Record World*, and *Cash Box*. Their first album "San Francisco/Hollywood" was named Disco Single of the Year by Billboard's Disco Forum Four, 1978.

The Trammps

The big excitement of the 1977-78 season was "Disco Inferno," courtesy of the Trammps, a bunch of guys who've been hanging out together since the 1960s when they made their first hit as the Volcanoes. Within the past three years, they have become the number one disco group in the country. Three Billboard International Disco Forums have named them the Disco Group of the Year.

"Disco Inferno," released early in 1977, was an eleven-

Trammps: Their "Disco Inferno" became disco dancers' theme song   COURTESY ATLANTIC RECORDS

minute LP disco number which hit all the rhythm and blues and popular music charts in the first week it was released. Within a month, the eleven-minute rendition had been shaved to a three-and-a-half minute single which also made all the charts.

The group started picking up awards all over the country shortly after it started doing disco with Atlantic Records, in 1976. Their first album, *Where the Happy People Go*, took all honors in 1976, and *Disco Inferno* was a smash the next year. In the early spring of 1977, the Trammps sold out their first major solo appearance in Manhattan. It was an unforgettable event, a five-hour disco dance celebration that attracted a crowd of 3,000 to New York's famed Roseland Ballroom.

The group has its musical roots in the Philadelphia sound, and their fifties/sixties vocal approach was the essence of disco long before the disco explosion of the seventies.

How come they're "Trammps"?

"Most of the guys were raised up on street corners," says leader Earl Young, "doing all kinds of crazy things and getting chased away by the man, hearing, 'All you'll ever be is a bunch of tramps.'"

Michael Zager's Band

Perhaps the most fun disco number of the 1977-78 season, this one had the disco freaks on the floor howling and hooting and waving their hands like Indians doing a rain dance.

The commotion was caused by Michael Zager Band's "Let's All Chant," issued by Private Stock Records, Ltd. The band was put together just to make the record, and to produce it, Zager brought together more than two dozen of the top "session players"—recording musicians—in New York.

The album originated when Zager's partner, Jerry Love, became aware that chanting was becoming very popular in discos around the country. He suggested that Zager, with co-writer Alvin Fields, write a song that would incorporate the chanting beat.

It turned out to be one of the most danceable albums in the deejays' record library, featuring everything from the latest

Michael Zager: He and his band had them squealing on the disco floor COURTESY PRIVATE STOCK

electronic innovations to a tribute to Walt Disney's films. The Disney bit was an eight-minute disco salute which whirled through such favorites as "Hi Ho," "Whistle While You Work," and "Give a Little Whistle." You haven't really lived until you've heard "When You Wish Upon a Star," done in disco style!

Zager himself was originally co-leader of the horn band, Ten Wheel Drive, and when that group split after four years of touring and recording, Zager turned to arranging, composing, and producing.

"Let's All Chant," began showing up on the deejay Top 10 lists as soon as the record became available. It incorporates just about every known disco chant, and an off-the-wall seventies-style chamber music break that is quite beautiful.

By the time the band has worked up to the lines: "your body/my body/everybody work your body" the whole room has been disco-fied.

Zager says his commitment is to make music that makes you feel good. As anyone who ever disco-ed to "Let's All Chant" can tell you, he succeeds.

Chic

"Chic," says *Webster's Dictionary*, is "smart elegance and sophistication . . . cleverly stylish . . . currently fashionable. . . ." Chic, in the world of disco music, is a group of musicians who manage to fit that description musically while turning disco dancers into a state of unchic frenzy at the same time.

It was Chic who produced the disco single, "Dance, Dance, Dance," that knocked the discophiles flat on both the East Coast and West Coast almost as soon as it was released. Its trademark: the occasional exclamations of "yowsah, yowsah, yowsah," reminiscent of the cheers of encouragement during the days of the dance marathons.

The group includes: Bernard Edwards, born in Greenville, North Carolina, and a New Yorker since the age of ten, a student at the High School of Performing Arts, and an all-round musician with extensive performing background. It was while he was working a day job at the post office that he met Nile Rodgers (whose girlfriend's mother worked at the post office, too). Nile was born on the Triboro Bridge en route to Queens General Hospital, was reared in Greenwich Village and Hollywood. He had moved musically from hard rock guitar through classical studies to jazz, and then Bernard turned him on to rhythm and blues.

Drummer Tony Thompson, who had spent a year with La Belle prior to meeting Bernard and Nile.

Norma Jean Wright, vocalist, who had started singing in church in Elyria, Ohio, and later gigged around the Ohio-Michigan-Indiana circuit for a few years. After graduating from Ohio State University, she made the move to New York City in early 1977, and met Bernard and Nile shortly afterward.

Chic: They made discophiles dance, dance dance
COURTESY ATLANTIC RECORDS

Soon after Bernard and Nile started collaborating on their own album, their tune "Dance, Dance, Dance" began catching the attention of several record companies, and before long, Chic had signed with Atlantic Records. "DDD" was the hit of the 1977-78 disco season.

"Disco is now an important portion of American music," says Bernard Edwards. "It's like going back to the old days of the dancing crazes, when the big band came to town, everyone got excited, all the kids showed up and they just danced and had a good time. We're not trying to deliver any heavy message, just entertainment. When you're off from work, come and see us and have a good time. No moral issues, no heavy problems—you just come to see us, have a good time, and split—that's it."

Yowsah, yowsah, yowsah.

Thelma Huston

After several false starts, Thelma Huston struck gold in more ways than one with her disco recording, "Don't Leave Me This Way." The record sold more than the magic one-million, and Thelma was nominated as Top Disco Artist and Female Pop Artist of the Year by *Billboard* magazine.

After years of going to the Grammy Award events and not even being mentioned, Thelma found that the success of "Don't Leave Me This Way" changed her life.

"It means, wow, I really do exist as a singer. I do count," she said recently.

A resident of Long Beach, California, Thelma credits Motown Records' creative head, Suzanne DePaz, with giving her career the thrust it needed. For it was DePaz who brought her "Don't Leave Me This Way." Thelma also credits disco for helping her career and hopes it lasts a long, long time. "I'd just hate to think of it as a craze," she says.

"I think disco is very underrated. Something very good is going on there. It gives a good psychological lift to people. You can go to a disco and be depressed or maybe not feeling so good, and you get there and the music takes over. You don't think about anything or dwell on your low mood. You go there to unleash all that pent-up energy."

Thelma has much to celebrate these days, but a little more than ten years ago, she was working full-time by day during the week, and full-time by night on weekends, to help support her two children. About that time, she started booking herself into clubs in the Long Beach area for $25 or $50 a night. It was at one of these club dates in a private disco—The Factory, which is now the famed Studio One—that she met Mark Gordon, who became her manager and steered her career in the professional direction it needed.

A native of Mississippi, Thelma moved when she was ten years old to Long Beach, where she attended Poly High School, graduating in the same class with tennis great Billie Jean King. She married her high school sweetheart, but the marriage ended after the second child was born.

A singer in high school, Thelma had moved on to sing with gospel groups, and made her first album in 1966 with The Art Reynolds Singers.

But it took the disco beat to finally give Thelma Huston the break she had always dreamed of.

Yvonne Elliman

After years in the music industry, Yvonne Elliman, top recording artist for Robert Stigwood Organization, is breaking out into the spotlight. In 1977, she won the Don Kirschner Rock Award as Best Female Vocalist; and she was nominated by *Billboard* magazine as that year's Top Vocalist in the Easy Listening category.

Yvonne left her native Hawaii when she was seventeen, and headed for London seeking work as a singer. Her first job was at a King's Road club, The Pheasantry, where, just like the lucky-break fairy tale of the movies, it happened that Tim Rice and Andrew Lloyd Webber, authors of *Jesus Christ, Superstar*, were in the audience. Yvonne was immediately hired to play the role of Mary Magdalene, and her poignant rendition of "I Don't Know How to Love Him" was soon being heard everywhere.

As a member of that now legendary production, Yvonne recorded the original album, which sold in the millions. She performed the role in major theaters throughout the world and appeared in the motion picture version of the play as well. For that performance, the Hollywood Foreign Press Association nominated her for the Golden Globe Award as Best Actress.

Believing that she was losing her own identity in the character of Mary, Yvonne decided to return to London, where she recorded another solo album; and then returned to America just as Eric Clapton was emerging from his self-imposed retreat. While Clapton was recording in Miami, Yvonne went to the studio to listen to him work—and Eric recruited her as the strong female vocalist he needed for the chorus in his "I Shot the Sheriff."

Later, when he formed his band, Yvonne became his female vocalist, and she toured and recorded with him for three years. But, although she enjoyed those years with Clapton, she was still determined to work on her solo career.

Signed to RSO Records, she recorded an album titled *Rising Sun*, but it wasn't until her second album, *Love Me*, that Yvonne really attracted notice as a solo artist. In addition to her success with that album—two singles hit the Top 20— Yvonne recorded "If I Can't Have You," written by the Bee Gees for the soundtrack of the Robert Stigwood production of *Saturday Night Fever*.

Like everything else associated with *Fever*, this single was a best seller, too. It is included on her most recent album, *Night Flight*, which includes songs written by Yvonne herself, and others—including Neil Sedaka.

Madleen Kane

Madleen Kane, who records for Warner Brothers, is a relative newcomer to the pop music scene—or any scene, for that matter, since she is only twenty years old. But her first album, *Rough Diamond*, lost no time climbing toward the top of the disco music charts.

The new disco chanteuse, however, had to pay her dues like everyone else. She worked as a model for a few years before she was able to do what she had always wanted to do.

"I have always wanted to sing," she says. "I used to sing in church."

When she was in her teens, Madleen had lived for a while in the home of model agent Eileen Ford and her family, and it was not long before she became a very successful model. But she didn't like doing it.

"I actually modeled to earn money for singing lessons," she says.

Later, she turned down a part in a movie with Jack Nicholson because she didn't want to live in Hollywood.

Madleen Kane, former model turned singing star
WARNER BROTHERS RECORDS

"Acting would be nice," she says, "as long as I would not become an object."

Madleen was born in the south of Sweden. Her father was a piano maker; her mother, an American from San Francisco; and her growing-up years were marked by overseas travel, music lessons, dance lessons—and luxury.

After her years of modeling and being "someone else" before the cameras, Madleen says she is determined from now on to be herself.

"Everyone thinks I'm so fragile," she says, "but I love speed, and to drive sports cars. Everyone imagines I am superficial, but I love reading and music, Mozart above all. Everyone thinks I am so vain, yet I hate putting on makeup."

When she's not turning down movie offers or making hit records on her first try, Madleen hangs out with Princess Caroline of Monaco and folks like that.

Tuxedo Junction

Tuxedo Junction is three dynamic young women who have revived and revitalized the sound of the Big Band, turning classics like "Chattanooga Choo Choo," "Rainy Night in Rio," and "Moonlight Serenade" into exciting disco hits. The blending of the melodies of the forties and fifties with the pulsating beat of disco has captured the dancing feet of people everywhere, and is making this group one of the "hottest" in the country.

Jamie Edlin, Jane Scheckter, and Jeannie Kauffman create the Tuxedo Junction sound. Jamie, lead singer and creator of the group, grew up listening to such Big Band greats as Artie Shaw, Tommy Dorsey, and Glenn Miller. She trained as a singer, dancer, and actress in her native St. Louis, and eventually moved to New York where she has appeared on the stage, both on and off Broadway. She finally landed in Los Angeles, after a Midwest tour, and it was there that she established her recording career.

Jane Scheckter grew up in Massachusetts, singing and dancing with Dinah Shore, Doris Day, and Carmen Miranda—"in my living room," she says. She earned a degree in design at

****

Casablanca, the name that's synonymous with "disco" in the recording business, doesn't buy albums or artists simply because they have a beat to dance to.

"We'll sign something whether or not it's disco, as long as we like it," says Larry Harris, senior vice-president and managing director of the recording company. "If it is disco, it's got a bit of an edge only because a lot of record companies still don't pay much attention to the disco market.

"We've become the number one disco label—and we intend to stay the number one disco label. But we're interested in other things as well."

****

Pratt Institute and worked as a designer in New York, Italy, France, Hong Kong, and India.

At the same time, she continued singing, and performed with Barry Manilow in his early years. She has appeared in off-Broadway shows and performed in her own nightclub in New York.

Jeannie Kauffman, Brooklyn-born, moved to California at the age of six, and grew up to act in summer stock and community playhouses in California and throughout the western United States. She once had the dubious distinction of playing the part of Arnold Horshak's mother in Gabe Kaplan's nightclub act based on "Welcome Back, Kotter," and for a while, she was even delivering singing telegrams in the Los Angeles area. Tuxedo Junction rescued her.

The group's first single, "Chattanooga Choo Choo," for Butterfly Records not only chugged up the charts in record time, but it made every disco dancer over forty feel right at home.

Roberta Kelly

A former Los Angeles resident, Roberta Kelly calls Munich, Germany, her home these days, but she has developed a legion of fans on both sides of the Atlantic.

She is especially well known in Europe, where she has been performing for the past five or six years. More than 35,000 people turned out to hear her at the Verona Music Festival in Italy where her hit recording of "Zodiac Lady" was the number one single for eighteen weeks. The Italians also named her Singer of the Year in 1978.

An accomplished record-producer in Germany, as well as a hit vocalist, Roberta had toured with Donna Summer for two and a half years before embarking on her solo career. Recently, she has developed a sophisticated disco style that is blended with the earthy energy of gospel music.

Recording for Casablanca, her recent album, *Gettin' the Spirit*, features some compelling disco numbers like "Oh Happy Day," "Speaking My Mind," and "Walking in the Shadow of His Light."

Pattie Brooks

Pattie Brooks can't remember a time when she didn't sing or work with music. Born in Fort Riley, Texas, to a military family, she traveled a lot—to Chicago, to Fort Knox, and then to Germany where she lived for four years. But always, she wanted to sing.

"I was always singing around the house . . . though I must say, opera was the music I really loved at that time, because I could really sing high," she told an interviewer. "Then I went on to jazz and sang along with Ella Fitzgerald records—I learned to scat. Next came rock. But I always had my own thing."

For a brief time, she worked as a PBX operator and with the phone company, but as she says, "I knew that wasn't going to be my bag."

Her bag, of course, has been vividly on display this year in her first solo album, *Love Shook* (for Casablanca) which shook 'em up on the disco floors this season.

"Disco is something I never thought I would be in, but—there I am," she says. "I love disco music."

Patti got her first chance to get into music professionally in 1968 with a spot singing on the "Smothers Brothers Show," and went on to sing with Henry Mancini's Young Generation, on Bobby Darin's TV series, and the "Pearl Bailey Show," among others.

When Donna Summer was planning her *I Remember Yesterday* LP, Pattie was hired to sing and to help acquire the background vocalists for the recording session. Pattie feels Donna was a great influence on her career, and the two became close friends.

Pattie loves to dance, so disco, she says, is right up her alley.

"It's exciting, I know for me, when I'm wound up and just want to get away from everything and everybody. Disco is a whole new entity. It will always be here. It might take a different form, but as long as people want to dance, you're going to have disco."

Alec R. Costandinos

Alec R. Costandinos is a composer-producer who created a contemporary disco version of Shakespeare's *Romeo and Juliet* and, in doing so, created one of the big hits of last disco season. "Romeo and Juliet," which blended a compelling rock beat with a flowing, poetic meter, was also an engineering "first," for it was one of the first 48-track recordings ever made.

During ten days of recording and mixing, Costandinos and his engineers at Trident Studios in London put a new coding system to the test, synch-ing two 24-track tape recorders to within 1/2,000 of a second.

For the past two and a half years, the charts in France have consistently listed Costandinos's songs, and as a prolific writer, he has also had his songs recorded by Paul Anka and Henry Mancini, among others.

Casablanca Records expects more excitement to come, for Costandinos is a man of many interests.

"I'm a musician, an expressionist . . . perhaps a little bit of everything," he says, "which makes me a good producer."

Leroy Gomez

Leroy Gomez, a native of Cape Cod, Massachusetts, is of Portuguese heritage, lives in Paris, and, with one disco album, *Santa Esmeralda*, has achieved international stardom.

One tune, "Don't Let Me Be Misunderstood," recorded as part of the album for Casablanca Record and FilmWorks, was a smash, created by updating a hit of the sixties with a catchy Latin disco arrangement. In France, it broke sales records as it soared to the top of the charts, and the tune made number one in Germany, Italy, Spain, and Holland. It goes without saying that it was dancing dynamite in the U.S. discos in 1978.

Gomez, who plays guitar and flute as well as saxophone, is in great demand as a session musician, and is currently also one of the hottest concert attractions in Europe. He was voted the Best Live Act of 1977 in France.

In the meantime, in America, the discotheques were among the first to pick up on the infectious rhythms of *Santa Esmeralda* as an import record. When it became available through Casablanca, the phenomenonal European success of "Don't Let Me Be Misunderstood" simply repeated itself.

Munich Machine

As any follower of the European music scene will tell you, the recording industry in Munich, Germany, is making that city one of the creative centers of the continent. Out of this scene grew the Donna Summer phenomenon, and the international reputation of her producers, Giorgio Moroder and Pete Bellotte.

Moroder, along with co-producer Bellotte, is the chief cog in the Munich Machine. Once he had assembled a gifted group of musicians to support and surround their recording stars, Moroder decided it was only logical that the musicians step out from behind the scenes and create an album of their own. The result was a blend of disco and funk, and the "Get on the Funk Train" track immediately became one of the hits on the disco charts.

One of the chief engineers of the Munich Machine sound is Dino Solera, who performs on flute and saxophone. An Italian transported to Munich, Dino is one of the most sought-after musicians in Europe.

Chris Bennett, a Californian, debuted with the Machine in "A Whiter Shade of Pale," which has also been popular on the disco floors.

The Beat Goes On

The music had begun at twelve; now it was after two, yet the swaying bodies on the floor had scarcely missed a beat. In his electronic hotbox in a corner of the room, the deejay once more nudged the turntables' variable speed to a higher pitch and faster pace. He had been working toward this moment all night long, riding the pulse of the dancers, mixing record after record so that each was a little faster, higher in pitch, and more intense, urging the dancers toward frenzy.

Under the glittering canopy of lights, the floor seemed to heave with the pounding of feet, and the air began to crackle with sheer physical energy. Then the room exploded. Cries and calls and a thousand wildly waving arms filled the air as the music virtually lifted the dancers off their feet and off the floor. It was a simmering, sizzling moment of pure primitive emotion. It was the essence of the disco experience.

The orchestrators of that experience are people many dancers never know and seldom see. They are the spinners, the disco jockeys, the men who make the music. Sitting in glass-enclosed booths high above the dancers, or hidden behind pillars or mirrors, or tucked away in darkened corners, these are the men who make the disco experience happen.

The disco deejay has to be a technical wizard of music and mood, a psychologist, a creative manipulator of other men's art, and a glutton for hard work. For the music at a disco never stops.

Hour after hour, hand in glove with the lighting-effects man, the deejay keys in on the mood of the crowd—choosing individual records, individual selections, to create the effect he wants. In smaller discotheques, the disc jockey may also be the lighting man, in which case he is a lot busier—but his goal is the same—to get the room going, to make people dance.

"You have to make people work," says François Dubonnet of New York New York, a former professional musician. "You have to make them try to lose a little bit of their self-consciousness, to take them away and slowly bring them to a point of ecstasy. If the music is not good, no matter how fabulous the disco, you have a nothing place."

"Sophisticated disco crowds really know their music," says Joel Jacobs of Les Mouches, a beautiful, mixed straight-gay disco located in a warehouse district near the Hudson River in Manhattan.

"You've got to give them the music they know and want to hear, and at the same time give them something exciting and new. Change, newness, surprise—you use them all to get the people on their feet and keep them there. I don't like to use the word 'control,' but a deejay really *can* do things with people."

After a while, it is hard to tell who are the puppets and who are the puppeteers. The dancers are dancing beneath the lights, the light man is dancing at his control panel, and the deejay is dancing at the turntables.

★★

Back in the sixties, when the Peppermint Lounge was a little club where people shook and quivered to the beat of The Twist, Richie Kaczor was a young music freak, growing up in Elizabeth, New Jersey, spending his allowance on black soul music, and dreaming of being a disco jockey.

In 1975, when the Peppermint Lounge became the Hollywood discotheque, Richie Kaczor was there, in the deejay's booth, blue-jeaned and T-shirted, and happily creating nightly frenzy. Today, he's the resident deejay at Studio 54, still a music freak, still happily dancing between the revolving turntables and stacks of discs, building up to the moment when he turns a thousand flailing strangers into a family of mad dancers. How does he do it?

"I take a song and I work it and work it and work it," he says, "until I'm practically under the wax."

★★

"It all has to work together," says Richie Kaczor of Studio 54. "Your music turns the light man on, what he does affects the deejay, what you both do turns the crowd on—and the people then turn *you* on!"

It all adds up to a moment, an hour, two hours and more of intense emotional excitement and physical release. It is the ultimate disco experience. It's what all those people outside the door are waiting for.

The DJ booth where the orchestration of discomania happens
1978 DISCOTHEKIN' NEWS/DOCUMENT ARCHIVES

Deejays at Work

There is more to making music than just putting records on a turntable—and "spinning" as it is known in the business, has become a fine art—part mechanics, part musicianship, and totally creative. Since disco music is nonstop, and part of the disco experience is that unremitting buildup to that explosive moment of release, the deejay must know more than the music, he must know his machinery.

The term most commonly heard when people start talking about disco deejays is "segue" (pronounced segg-way), and what it means as far as the dancer is concerned is that the music moves from one song to another without a break in the beat, with no discernible change of key and pace. In ballroom and conventional dance settings with live bands, dancers are used to having the music stop.

But there is nothing more disconcerting on the disco floor than to hear, or feel, a pause or break between songs. It's the loudest silence in the world. It throws dancers off their pace, slows the action, and to use a disco phrase—it "really messes up the floor."

In the more musically sophisticated crowd, the most important attribute of a deejay is a finely honed technique. At a gay disco, for instance (gay men are known as the most discerning listeners and dancers on the disco scene), the deejay's job is tough.

"Make the tiniest little bobble, something no one else would notice, and they give you a look," one veteran reports. "And you really make a bad segue—they'll walk right off the floor!"

The average disco crowd is not this harsh, but while they may not know what is wrong, they know very well that something is not right. After a while, they just don't come back.

The number of disco deejays is growing as fast, if not faster, than the number of discotheques in the country—and that is growing like wildfire, thanks to *Saturday Night Fever*. There are outstanding deejays everywhere—some well known in an entire region, some known only to the cognoscenti who patronize their clubs.

★★

Sharon Lee, deejay at Scaramouche in Miami, was picked by *Billboard* Magazine Disco Forum as the top female deejay in the United States in 1977.

Sharon White, deejay at Sahara, a women's disco in New York, was winner of the first annual Deejay of the Year Award, in 1978, presented by the Association of Women Deejays.

★★

It would be hard for anyone to pick the best deejays in the country, although *Billboard* magazine tries to do it each year at its International Disco Forum. But it is not difficult to select two names that everyone on the disco scene knows, respects, and concedes the championship title to—Tom Savarese and Bobby DJ Guttadaro.

Both are young and tops in their own field, but their names are still relatively unknown outside the field of disco and recorded music. Here, for the benefit of those who have never met them, is a closer look at a couple of legends.

Tom Savarese

"I'm a performer," Tom Savarese once shouted as he worked the twin turntables, a sound-mixing board and a digital computer for an electronic light show in the lucite deejay booth at 12 West in New York City. "I'm a performer, and these people out there had better know they're being entertained!"

They knew it—and disco dancers have known it for all the years Tommy has been spinning. He was the only disc jockey ever to get a standing ovation every Friday and Saturday night.

For two years—1976 and 1977—Savarese and his friend, Bobby DJ Guttadaro, have shared honors as the Number One Deejay of the Year, named by *Billboard* magazine's International Disco Forum. Volatile and temperamental, Savarese, thirty-four, conducts a personal compaign to make the world—and especially disco owners—aware that a discotheque disc jockey is not just "some guy spinning records," but an artist and an entertainer.

The deejay cannot simply be a technician, he says. "If you don't notice the disc jockey, then what is the purpose of being there?"

What makes him unique is his chemistry—blending records, making disco freaks scream and sweat as they stay glued to the dance floor. He uses his own record library, and his program is different every night—blending rock, pop, mood albums, and singles.

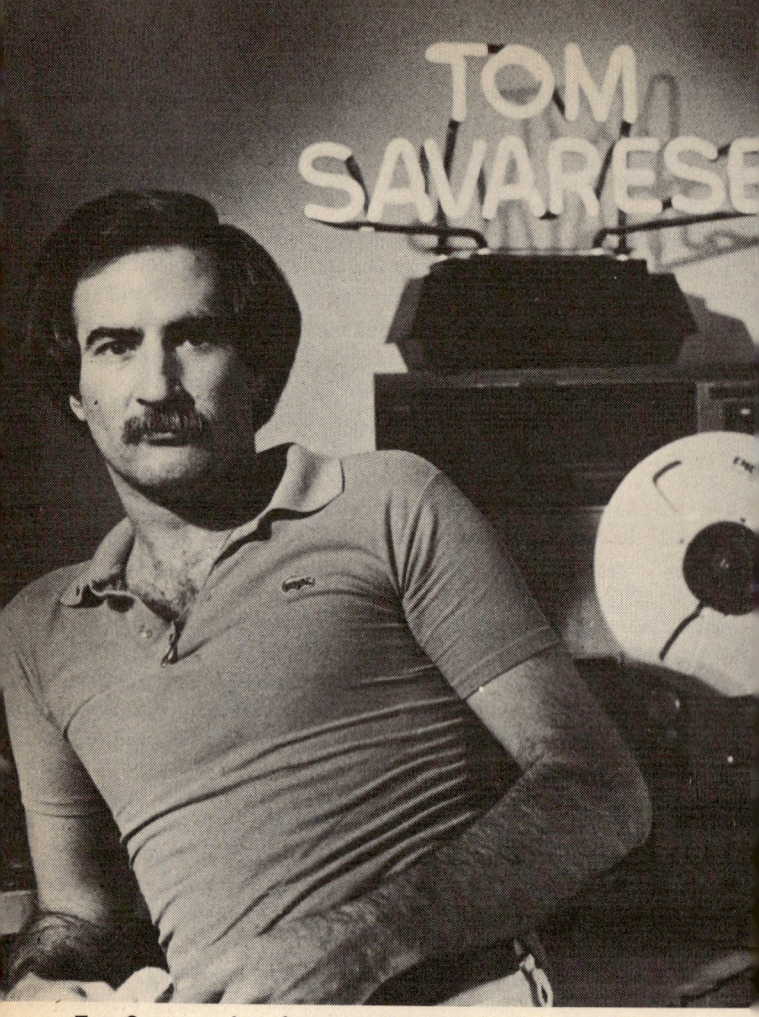

Tom Savarese: A performer at the turntables

Savarese's ability to blend musical riffs, underlying beats, and strobe lights to create a special kind of disco atmosphere is self-taught. A friend had asked him one night to play records at the now-defunct Club Cabaret, and he was hooked.

"Those days were a disaster," he recalls with a laugh. But,

working through trial and error during the days when discos were new and the exception to the entertainment rule, he developed the technique which has made him a name among all deejays in the country. He has run the gamut from the pits to public mid-Manhattan clubs, to private clubs where the chic and celebrity types hang out.

"I went at it to be the best, and best known," he admits. "It satisfied something in me that had to be accomplished."

Still working as a disco deejay in the top clubs, Savarese is also doing recording work, following his mix of the top disco hit "Dance, Dance, Dance." For the first time in the history of the recording industry, credit for music coordination was given equal billing to the song title on "TK Disco Party"—an album Tom Savarese mixed.

He is also program director of Disconet, a company which provides pre-mixed disco programming for discotheques and deejays throughout the country.

Bobby DJ Guttadaro

"The man's got ears."

That's what they say in the trade about Bobby DJ Guttadaro, the thirty-year-old, soft-spoken disc jockey with neatly trimmed hair and eyeglasses, who has been described as "a master of controlled frenzy."

Moviegoers may recall that he's the man who mixed the soundtrack for the Casablanca/Motown movie, *Thank God It's Friday*. It was Marc Paul Simon of Casablanca who asked him to do the job, and when he accepted, the record company flew him out to California. It took him six months. He read the script, decided what kind of music was necessary for particular parts of the film, and then selected the artists he wished to perform the required songs. The actual filming of the movie and the recording sessions were done simultaneously.

In 1977, the Billboard International Disco Forum named him the top deejay in the country. He had been tops in New York for many years before that.

"Some people think all you have to do is throw on a fast record and people will dance to it," says Guttadaro. "That's

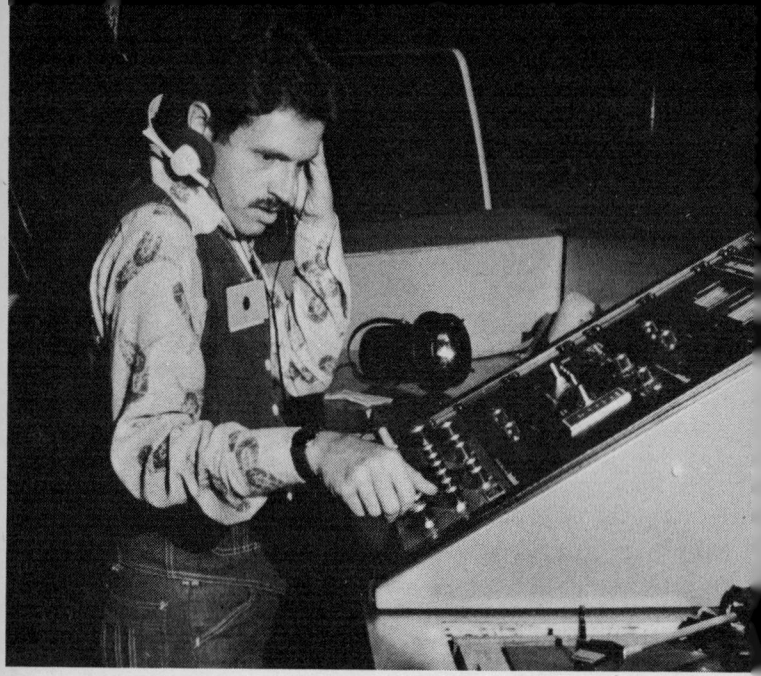

Bobby DJ Guttadaro: Ex-pharmacist is country's top music mixer
1978 DISCOTHEKIN' NEWS/DOCUMENT ARCHIVES

nonsense. Being a disco disc jockey is like being an entertainer on stage. You whip the crowd up, you bring them down, and then you whip them up again."

Guttadaro has whipped them up at some of the top discos in the country: at the Zodiac, one of New York City's first discos, at Le Jardin, at New York New York, Infinity, and Ice Palace.

In the summer of '73, Bobby DJ was a twenty-five-year-old pharmacy student whose extensive record collection led him to a job as a deejay at Fire Island's Ice Palace. He dropped out of pharmacy, although he has his license—something he once called his insurance.

"If I want to, I can retire and become a pharmacist in Florida."

He will probably not be retiring for a year or two. He has offers from record companies to do re-mixes, still does gigs at discotheques. Guttadaro also mixes disco music for Disconet, which provides taped programs for disco-deejays, giving them not only a brief tape break during the evening but providing them with some of the top record-mixing skills in the country.

A native of Brooklyn, Guttadaro attended parochial schools and is a graduate of the Brooklyn College of Pharmacy. He was one of the first deejays to make record companies realize that a disco jockey can push a hit over the top, since many of the frenzied dancers at discos march into record stores the next day to buy what the deejay played the night before.

When working clubs, Guttadaro does not plan his music selections ahead of time, choosing instead to rely on the vibrations he gets from the crowd. A disc jockey has to have a sixth sense, he says, so that he can pick up on what the audience wants, lifting the crowd from one energy level to another, bringing them down a little, and then starting to climb again.

As America's number one deejay, Guttadaro has, over the years, built up his own cult following, and where Bobby DJ goes, many dancers follow.

"I love what I do," he says. "I love music. I guess I must have vinyl in my veins."

Disco at Home

They can make a mood, shape a party, and turn your home, your garage, or anywhere else into a disco for a day—or night. They are the mobile disc jockeys who have been making parties with their sound equipment and record collections for a number of years, and who find that the current disco phenomenon has turned good business into booming business and there is no peak in sight.

Part of the charm of the mobile deejay is the current love affair with disco. But part of it also lies in the fact that the disc jockey is often cheaper to hire than a live band. For anywhere from $150 to $300 and up, the mobile deejays will bring in their turntables, their speakers, their lights, and their records to provide a disco party in your house.

Norman Dolph, of Stoy, a New York firm, is one of an estimated 1,500 mobile dejays who are making music around the country these days, providing everything from rock to swing, from country-western to golden oldies at every kind of party from sweet sixteens and bar mitzvahs to weddings and back again.

Stoy's mobile equipment is fastened in place with aircraft connectors so that it will stay locked, despite vibrations or guests tripping the light fantastic over it. Such precautions, says Dolph, prevent the two most serious things that can happen to a mobile disc jockey: (1) permanent silence, and (2) temporary silence.

Slim Hyatt

A discreet little advertisement in a magazine announces the services of a mobile disc jockey, Slim Hyatt, who, to most disco devotees, needs no introduction. Hyatt is known as the first disco deejay on the scene, and today is one of the busiest around.

Hyatt began his career in 1962 at the famed Le Club in New York City, one of the "in" clubs of the sixties. Being the first disco deejay produced problems that neither the club owners, nor Hyatt, had anticipated. Local 802 of the Musicians Union in New York picketed Hyatt when he was spinning at Shepheard's, another (and still) successful "first" disco. Music on records, the union maintained, was putting live musicians out of work. It is an argument that continues to rage today.

"But the picket was a nice fellow," says Hyatt. "They only sent one, and he was the same one every night; he just sat with me and drank coffee while we talked about music."

Hyatt's work today takes him around the world. He has spun records in London, on the French Riviera, in Puerto Rico—and in Detroit, Miami, and Los Angeles.

In the New York area, he plays primarily for private parties, and his bookings have included the Sherry Netherland Hotel, the Waldorf, and the New York State Ballet Theater.

This deejay, says an admirer, is a man who can put songs by Sammy Davis, Frank Sinatra, and Barry White in a set together and make them sound as though they had recorded it that way.

After more than sixteen years behind the turntables, Hyatt

regards his disco deejaying with cool professionalism, as a job. But he admits, it has its moments.

"There are times when they have to force me to shut off the music when the party's going well. If the people are good, I enjoy the work."

London Records' national disco promotion man, Billy Smith, picks the disco deejays most important in breaking (introducing) a new disco record:

Jim Burgess, New York City
John Luongo, Boston
Kevin Burke, New York
John Hedges, San Francisco
Manny Slali, Hollywood
Roy Thode, New York
Richie Kaczor, New York
Richie Rivera, New York
A. J. Miller, Hollywood
Wayne Geftman, Philadelphia
Howard Metz, Dallas
Bo Crane, Miami
Howard Merritt, New York
Billy Stooke, Boston
Louis Padeira, San Juan
Vince Michaels, Washington, D. C.
Marty Angelo, Buffalo
Jack Witherby, Phoenix
Marty Dow, Key West, Florida
Paul Poulos, New York
Gary Larkin, Pittsburgh
Mort Christensen, Cleveland
Ken Smith, Houston
Bill Kennedy, Philadelphia

Creating a Disco Hit

Discomania may be a product of a hit movie and a new itch to dance, but discos themselves are the children of technology. It is technology that makes disco music systems so exciting, that makes a disco record sound the way it does, that creates the illusions, the lighting, and the special effects that are essential to the disco experience. Musicians, lighting engineers, and designers are the new discothechnologists. Their numbers are few—but growing fast.

To most people listening to a disco record, it would seem that quite a convention of musicians and vocalists had all converged on a recording studio for one giant recording session.

It doesn't happen that way. A popular music record today is not a group performance by a lot of people. It is an electronic mix of a lot of performances, done separately and at different times. It's called multitrack overdubbing, and this is how it works:

Each performance is recorded on a separate track—you might have twenty-four or more. The drum portion of the song may be on one track, the strings on another. Every musician listens on earphones to what has been recorded before while he sings or plays against those recorded performances. In the studio, as the master recording is being made, a vocal is added, another . . . another . . . an effect is brought in here, a Moog synthesizer there . . . bells, chants . . . whatever else you may hear on the record you finally buy.

The artist who created the song in the first place can thus create the final group performance and, hopefully, a top-of-the-charts best-selling record at the same time.

This is what Peter Brown—composer, musician, and singer—did when he produced his hit disco number, called "Dance with Me," for the TK Record company, one of the largest disco firms in the country.

An artist—musical or electronic—can mix as many tracks of vocals and instruments as he feels are necessary. And this kind of mixing and re-mixing can be done at any time. An

Peter Brown: A master of the over-dub technique
HOWARD BLOOM ORGANIZATION

original recording can be broken down into separate tracks all over again and then reassembled into a totally new-sounding production.

The mixer may speed up or slow down some of the original sections; they can be extended, intensified, dropped out all together—and the complete master recording brings one record together with another so sweetly, so smoothly, that the beat remains absolutely the same during the transition. A good mixer can even bring two records together in the middle of a phrase or break, and you wouldn't know it hadn't originally been done that way.

Tom Moulton, a mixing wizard, does this so brilliantly that

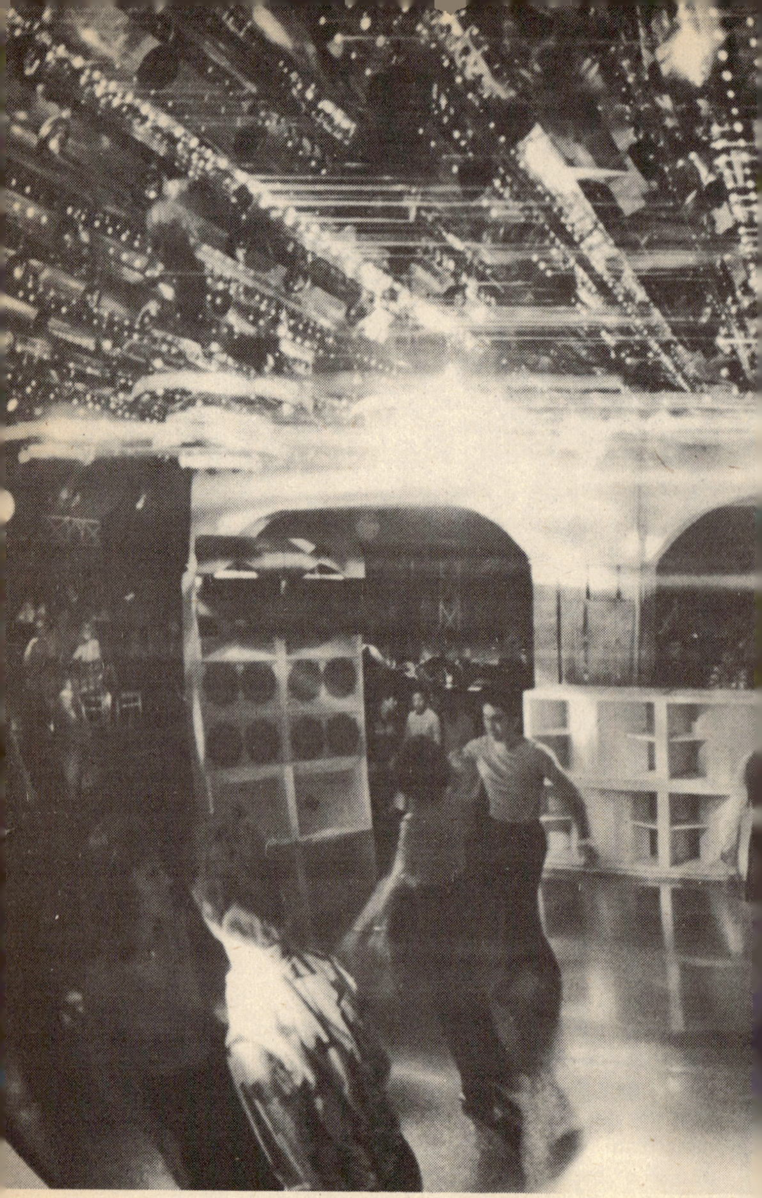

Limelight, Miami, Florida (1977)
PHOTO: RITCH BARNES, COURTESY OF L. SILVERMAN

record companies for whom he mixes carry his imprimatur on the label: "A Tom Moulton Mix." To record buyers who know their music and their electronics, that spells quality.

Lighting Pioneers

Larry Silverman, a soft-spoken man who wears steel-rimmed glasses and a modest manner, probably knows more than any one person has a right to know about electronics, computers, and all the other technology that goes into what he calls "specialized electronic entertainment systems for discotheques." Silverman, an MIT graduate and a pioneer in the disco lighting scene, most recently was a lighting consultant on the Robert Stigwood-Paramount Pictures production of *Saturday Night Fever*. In addition, he supplied the disco lighting and sound and the control installations for *Thank God It's Friday*.

He thinks discos are going to be around for a long time.

"I draw a parallel between the disco business and the movie business," he says. "They are both mass entertainment based on technology. In the first twenty years of the movies' history, everybody thought it was a fad and that it was going to go away. And then sound came along, and everybody said that sound wouldn't last. It took thirty or forty years, but the movies became a real industry.

"I think there is a similar phenomenon in disco. Sound and music are a basic part of American life, and the phenomenon of dancing as public entertainment goes back as far as you want to look. So you look at a discotheque, and what do you have—you have people enjoying music in any way that they can, and people enjoying dancing in a public format.

"That's mass entertainment and that's technology—and that gives you the elements of a continuing industry or business."

Silverman, who has been involved, one way or another, in the design of some 2,000 discotheques to date, says that all of the technology that makes the disco phenomenon possible has developed out of the space program—the greatest single impetus for technology in this country in the last fifty years. It was one of the major forces in developing miniaturization.

"The integrated circuits that are used in discotheques were developed for the space programs," says Silverman. "If it weren't for NASA, you wouldn't have Studio 54."

Silverman and Billboard Publications, Inc., have just launched StarStream, a videotape that projects pictures and images on disco walls and floors. Soon, he says, we'll have video-disc, which will let us all play our own disco effects at home.

Disco Environmentalists

The president of Design Circuit, Inc., New York, Robert Lobi, one of the top disco technologists in the country, is a former rock guitarist who used to pick up a little extra money by working the lights for the other acts on the concert tour. He found himself more interested in the lights than he was in the music.

It was Lobi and his associates who designed Infinity, the first disco to use neon and to have a light show in conjunction with the music. What they did, say the designers, was create the concept of an orchestra of light which a light man could play like a musical instrument to turn dancers into whirling dervishes and keep them on the floor all night.

Design Circuit's most recent disco is Scaramouche, in Miami, one of the most sophisticated they have ever done, says the man whose company has already created New York New York, the new Copacabana disco, and the new Shepheard's in New York as well as many discos in Europe.

"What you are doing when you design a discotheque," says Lobi, "is creating an environment—an artificial environment. And, as in the environment of nature, everything has to work in harmony, otherwise there are abrasions. Since you are dealing with a man-made environment, you run the risk of it being harsh, even sterile. A discotheque should be a 'harmony trip.'"

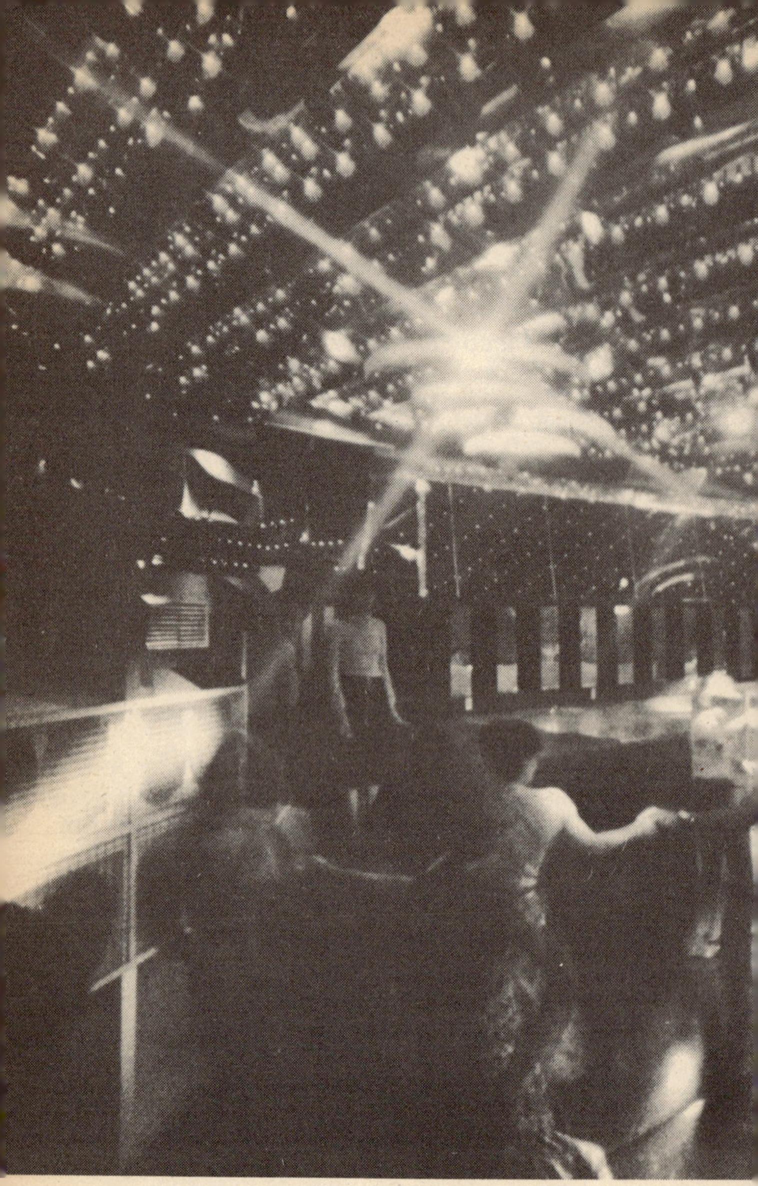

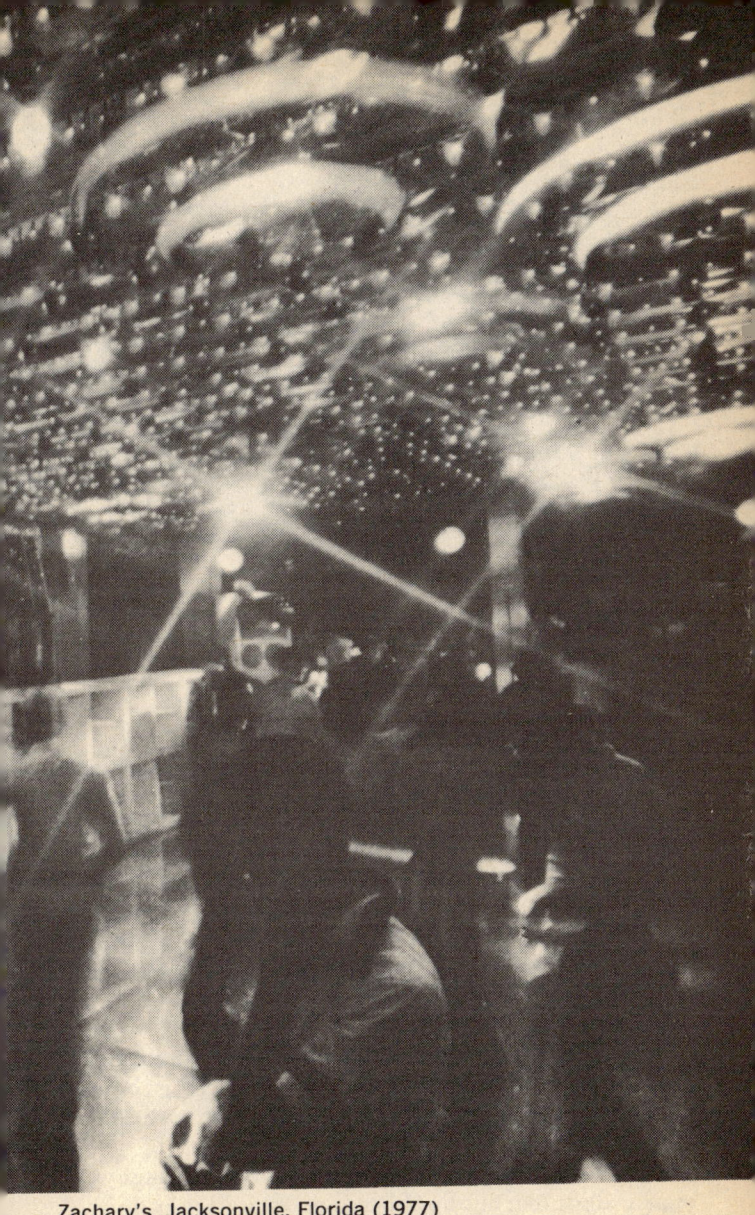

Zachary's, Jacksonville, Florida (1977)
PHOTO: RITCH BARNES, COURTESY OF L. SILVERMAN

Mirror balls and disco lights make the magic

That Mystifying Mist

The disco beat goes on—harder, faster, crazier—and all at once, fountains of smoke pour from the ceilings, and a misty fog begins to rise from the floor.

Ever wonder how they do that?

It's easy, say the youthful electronic magicians at Design Circuit, Inc., which has designed special effects for some of the world's most exciting discotheques. All you do is drop a chunk of dry ice into a machine, then jet hot water on it at a temperature of about 160 degrees.

Presto! Steam—or fog.

Since there's a very firm lid on top of the dry ice chamber, the fog is forced to find its way out through ducts and channels that open in the ceiling or around the dance floor—which is exactly what the designers had in mind.

A fog effect that lasts about twenty to thirty minutes would require about four hundred pounds of dry ice per load.

And you thought it was magic!

Turn-on lighting at Picassio's, near Los Angeles, California
PHOTO AND LIGHTING BY DESIGN CIRCUIT, INC.

Night Fever

"Saturday Night Fever" was born in June, 1976, on the cover of *New York Magazine*, which announced the "Tribal Rites of the New Saturday Night," an article by Nik Cohn. Cohn was the self-described "man in a tweed suit," the "journalist from Manhattan" who had spent many nights and weekends in Brooklyn exploring and reporting on the disco life-style of the new generation of the seventies.

The events, Cohn said in an introduction to his article, were factual; some of them he had personally seen or participated in, others had been told to him. The names of the principal characters had been changed.

Cohn's article concentrated on one group of friends whom he called the "Faces"—more than a clique, not quite a gang, growing up in Bay Ridge, Brooklyn, living through uninspired days at uninspiring jobs, waiting for the weekend and the chance to let loose, to explode.

The article caught the eye of producer Robert Stigwood who promptly bought the screen rights; and John Travolta, who had just been signed by Stigwood for a three-picture deal, seemed a natural choice for the role of the central "Face" of Cohn's story. Screenwriter Norman Wexler, two-time Oscar nominee for his screenplay for *Joe* and for *Serpico*, was chosen to adapt the article to the screen.

The star and pivotal personality of the Faces in Nik Cohn's article was called Vinnie, a boy who found his release and his identity on the disco dance floor. In Wexler's screenplay, Vinnie became Tony Manero. And behind that fictional character, whose inchoate yearnings and youthful drives have caught the soul and spirit of millions of the youth of the seventies, are three very real personalities:

Travolta at '78 Oscar ceremonies; he'd been nominated for "best performance by an actor in a leading role" in *Saturday Night Fever*.   WIDE WORLD PHOTO

Eugene "Tony" Robinson, disco king and delivery boy
Deney Terrio, disco king and dancer
John Travolta, disco king and actor

The Three Faces of Tony Manero:
Eugene Robinson

"I talked to this man on the phone. He said he was a writer and was searching for a person like me. That there were other guys that could dance fantastic, but that he was looking for the 'ultimate face' . . . he said to me, 'You go out there and prove to me that you are this person.' And I poured everything into his hand."

Eugene Robinson was only eighteen when Nik Cohn made that phone call: eighteen years old and a high school dropout; eighteen years old and working as a delivery boy in a paint store in Bay Ridge, Brooklyn, to help support his parents and five sisters and three brothers. That was more than two years ago and the beginning of a phenomenon that became *Saturday Night Fever*, the bench-mark film that fueled an epidemic of discomania from coast to coast. It was a movie that made John Travolta a star, made millionaires of the Bee Gees, who did the music, and is making Paramount Pictures and the Robert Stigwood Organization very rich indeed.

But two years after that phone call, the real "Tony Manero" was still working as a delivery boy in Brooklyn, glad to have been a part of film history, yet feeling that the opportunities it had brought so many others have just begun to touch his life.

Muscular, fair-haired, very pale, and a bit breathless, Robinson took a break from his six-to ten-hour dance practice to talk with us in the LeTang's Studio on Broadway. He had been preparing for a forthcoming appearance at Caesar's Palace in Las Vegas as part of a gala disco show preceding the Larry Holmes–Ken Norton fight for the World Boxing Council's Heavyweight Championship.

Eugene Robinson had become Tony Robinson. The disco king was going pro.

"This guy, the writer, Cohn, he said he was looking for the ultimate face . . . I showed him a real person, a way of living," says Robinson. "You can't be a king of disco if you just can dance. You've got to be able to fight, meet women, have charisma, handle yourself at the bar . . . and work six days a week at a hard job. You do all that and you can dance like nobody else . . . that's a king of disco.

"That night, I danced solo. When I dance, I bring the music out through my body, and everybody dwells on me. That night, I was doing The Walk, and everybody got off the floor and watched. That don't usually happen. But that night, I was so up-headed, I could've done anything.

"I didn't mean to dance that way. It just happened. People were cheering me. Cohn said I was the face he was looking for. A photographer who was with him even took a picture of me with my friend which was used for the sketch in the magazine." (Note: The drawing in the magazine article is unmistakably Robinson.)

"Later on, when the movie people came to make the picture there at the Odyssey, I danced as an extra and they paid me $400. But as the picture was going on, I was getting uncomfortable. I didn't mind being an extra. But more and more, I didn't like the way I was being treated. I felt the friction between those who wanted to treat me fair as the real Tony Manero, and those who wanted to brush me off."

"Travolta—he was a nice guy. He said once that 'Eugene is the character I played. This is a character who comes out of the water for air every once in a while.' Maybe I'm like that.

"During the filming breaks, we'd talk. He was the only gentleman on the set. He saw what was happening, but there wasn't anything he could do about it."

By the time the film was finished, the relations between some film company people and the boy whose life-style they were filming were so strained that Robinson did not even attend the cast party. He was not invited to the preview. But he has seen *Saturday Night Fever* three times, and each time, he paid his own way.

"I like the dancing and the music," he says. "And that scene in my room where I am combing my hair and getting ready to go out is really me. I felt like they were in my room when I saw that. Everything the guy does is me."

Saturday Night Fever has not improved Robinson's bank balance, as it has others', but it is making a difference in his life.

"There's only a couple of ways you can get out of Brooklyn. You go to school, get an education, and you get a good job. Or, you drop out of school and get a job, and go to clubs, meet a girl, and get married. I didn't know what I wanted to do, or be, when I grew up. Now I know I want to be a professional dancer, to have an act. My old job in the paint store kept me fit, and dancing is good for your body. Dancing professionally is a little harder. It's like starting all over again."

Today, Robinson is hard at work on his professional dance career.

The Three Faces of Tony Manero:
Deney Terrio

Deney Terrio is a Floridan who danced his way through junior high school and high school in Titusville, Florida, and finally, in 1971, danced his way to California where he sought fame and fortune as an entertainer—and earned his living by winning dance contests in the clubs around Los Angeles. Then, in 1976, Deney met John Travolta. From his parents' home—where he frequently returns for "rest and recuperation" with his family (two sisters and a brother), Terrio talks about what it has meant to be the dancer who taught John Travolta to dance.

Terrio: Well, to begin with, I never was a teacher, and I sure don't want to go into teaching now. There's 900 people claiming they taught John Travolta and they are all teaching disco classes. So I don't want to even be closely related to that.

KH: But you really did, didn't you?

Terrio: Do what?

KH: Taught John Travolta to dance.

Terrio: I sure did. I taught him everything. Well, all the stuff that counts. The knee drops, the splits on the floor, the tango hustle . . .

KH: Travolta has said he always liked to dance. So, at least he could move when you met him, right?

Terrio: Yes.

KH: Is he a graceful person?

Terrio (hesitating): Mmmm. No.

KH: So he had to *work* at his dancing?

Terrio: He worked with me for three and a half months. Remember, basically, John's an actor. . . . I had met his agent and he had told me that John was working on a dance movie and he was interested in the disco thing I did. . . . So, I met John, and he started talking to me, and I started telling him about all these crazy steps I'd been working on for years. . . . And he said, well, that sounds great, and why didn't the three of us—John, his agent, and me—get together. So, they started paying me on a weekly basis.

KH: How much work did that involve?

Terrio: We would work three nights a week, three hours a night. I didn't use just my own material. I would watch other dancers, and would take steps from them and teach them to John. That was my job. I wanted to make John Travolta look like Valentino—cocky, brash, but a lover, one that loves hard. . . . And I had a girl that used to stretch him, because another one of my jobs was to make sure he didn't hurt himself. Can you imagine teaching a guy to do those knee drops and splits without hurting himself?

KH: But at any rate, he was a fair dancer to start with?

Terrio: As a matter of fact, there were many nights that people were dancing that John wouldn't even get up on the floor. John was very paranoid at first.

KH: I suppose because he was in a totally different sphere.

Terrio: I give him credit, because I know what he went through just to make that movie. He went through losing a lot of confidence in himself. At first he used to ask—he felt so awkward at doing it, because he would see me there doing it and he would say 'Why don't I look like that?' And then all of a sudden, he started keeping up with me . . . his timing was getting there and he started feeling it, and then he started knowing that he had it.

KH: He certainly looks like a dancer now.

Terrio: Right . . . and now he can't get away from it.

KH: I don't think he's that anxious to be a dancer.

Terrio: No. No, he's not. And I tell everybody that he really isn't. He loves dancing . . . but he's said it in interviews, he's not that guy. That was a part he played.

KH: Were *you* that guy?

Terrio: Well, in a way, some of that movie was my world because when I started getting into dancing, I started laying carpets at one point, just to make a living. I was a carpet layer in the daytime, and I would sit around down on my knees, in old torn-up jeans and a growth of beard, and none of the girls would look at me. And then at night, I would shave and dress up and go dancing in a contest somewhere and I would make a little money on top of it. And my social life was great!

KH: So the disco-king part of the film was your experience?

Terrio: Well—the story in the film that is my story begins when John walks into the disco. That's when my world started. When he walked in, and everybody's going "Hey!" you know, "Hey, Tony!" because that's what used to happen to me, because I had won the state singles dance contests . . . and these people all knew me. . . .

KH: A real *Saturday Night Fever* scene . . .

Terrio: Well, at the time I was working with John and with the Stigwood people, *Saturday Night Fever* was called "Tribal Rites of the New Saturday Night," which was a magazine article by Nik Cohn. Now was there any mention of a dance contest in that article?

KH: Well, no.

Terrio: Right. Well, where do you think that came from?

KH: It must have come from someone who might have won a dance contest. Like Deney Terrio?

Terrio: Right. There were five original people that worked on *Saturday Night Fever*—and this was all out on the coast, long before they went to New York—and that was Norman Wexler, the screen writer; John Travolta; myself; a representative from Robert Stigwood; and John Avildsen, the director who did *Rocky*. So one night we go to this club, and Wexler comes in with about ten packs of cigarettes and notebooks hanging out of his arms and he sat down questioning me and questioning me for hours . . . and I told him about how the girls used to come up to me . . . and I told him about grabbing two girls up and dancing and I told him how if you had to be the disco king, you had to show it, that there were little groups and each group had its own great dancer . . . and I told him about the dance contest and how they would give trophies and a cash prize—

KH: Sounds familiar to anyone who's seen the movie.

Terrio: One time Travolta publicly gave me credit, but the poor guy is caught between people, and which way is he gonna go?

KH: But a lot of the things Travolta has said in interviews sound like things you have told me were your experiences.

Terrio: Look, John is a nice guy, he really is. He is really a decent person. But he's an actor, not a dancer, so when people get on to him and ask him "Where did you learn," he doesn't know where to go with the question. What's he gonna say, "Deney Terrio taught me everything I know"?

The Three Faces of Tony Manero:
John Travolta

"Vincent was the very best dancer in Bay Ridge. . . ." Thus begins Nik Cohn's description of the young Brooklyn American who has become this generation's Everyman, who sheds his blue collar every Saturday night to don one of his fourteen floral shirts and become the absolute ruler and king of the disco dance floor. This is Vinnie, who became, on film, the country's most famous working man since "Marty"—Tony Manero of *Saturday Night Fever*, who once thought about the future and decided he wanted to be "a star—someone like a hero."

Of the three faces of Tony Manero, only John Travolta's is that of a star.

For John Travolta, the actor, Tony Manero, the delivery boy, was a "character," a "challenge," and now is ancient history. The talented twenty-four-year-old TV teen idol, whose performance in *Saturday Night Fever* helped set the whole country dancing, long ago fled the gritty streets of Bay Ridge, Brooklyn. Ten days after he finished filming *Fever* he was dancing again—this time for the filming of *Grease*, a movie which was released last spring. And this fall, moviegoers saw him in another film, *Moment by Moment*, in which he plays a delivery boy, opposite Lily Tomlin.

Becoming "Tony Manero" for the film that made him a star was not easy for Travolta, who had had little experience with the life-style and characters he was to portray.

"I couldn't identify myself with this man," he said, "except that I enjoy dancing."

So Travolta, who grew up in Englewood, New Jersey, began hanging around discotheques in Brooklyn.

"A lot of what I put on the screen came from guys I met there. They were extreme in their personalities. I'd see where their values were—where women and dancing stood in their lives. They all had one thing in common—they wanted to get out of Brooklyn."

The role of Tony Manero also demanded months of physical preparation on Travolta's part; his background as a dancer was limited to a year of summer stock and a role in the Broadway musical *Over Here*.

"When I got this film, I danced in a studio three hours a night for five months. Then, after the lessons, I'd go to the discos and try out my stuff. In New York, I went a couple of times and hung out at different discos. I spent a couple of days in Brooklyn with Norman Wexler, who wrote the script. I spent a lot of time talking to some of the kids, and I met some characters who are absolutely incredible, that I used in the movie. I thought, if Tony Manero's supposed to be the best, I want to be the best."

One of the high spots of the film was Travolta's electrifying solo on the disco dance floor—something that rarely happens to real disco kings—not even in Brooklyn's Odyssey 2001. John, the actor, explained:

"I had to enforce that scene. They were basing this movie on his being the best dancer, and he didn't have a solo. I had to prove to the audience that he was the best."

What about people who don't know Brooklyn? Can they go away from the movie believing that the boys who grow up there, boys like Tony Robinson and the others who hung out at the Odyssey in those days, are really like that?

★★★

Everyone knows what happened to John Travolta after he won that disco dancing contest in *Saturday Night Fever*. He went on to *Grease*, and later, to Lily Tomlin, and who knows where it will all end.

But the dancer whom he "beat"—a professional dancer by the name of Joseph Pugliese, of South Brooklyn, learned something from the experience—but it wasn't about dancing.

"I learned never to assume anything," said Pugliese, who had worked up his routine for that dance in a week. He thought he would get screen credit for his work. His contract didn't say so.

He didn't.

★★★

"I can't make a statement for the masses," says Travolta, "but I know what appeals to me. I try to duplicate life as I see it, and I tend to give common reality with other people. The character strikes close to home. Watching Tony, I saw loneliness, frustration; I saw everything people deal with in real life. Nothing glamorous about his personality, he's neither macho nor withdrawn, heroic or antiheroic. He is universally identifiable."

Although John is the youngest of a large Italian Catholic family of six children, the resemblance to Tony stops there. John's father is a retired semiprofessional football player and co-owner of a tire store. His mother, Helen, was an actress, a director, and a high school theater arts teacher who had studied at Columbia University. John started his career at the age of nine in the summer stock production of *Bye Bye Birdie*. When he was sixteen, he talked his father into letting him quit school and try for a career in the theater. At the age of seventeen, he moved to Manhattan.

"The wonderful thing about my parents," he says, "is that they gave us confidence. We were the best. Whether we were or not, this energy came out of us as creative talent."

Travolta gets a little steamed when people suggest that things have come to him too easily, that he hasn't suffered enough for his art.

"It's bull that you have to suffer to be a creative artist," he says angrily. "Pain only gets in the way. Suffering only makes you less creative."

John knows about suffering. In the middle of the production of *Saturday Night Fever*, he suffered the profoundest sorrow of his twenty-three years. The only love of his life, Diana Hyland, died in his arms of cancer, at the age of forty-one. A blond Grace Kelly type, Diana had played the minister's alcoholic wife on the TV "Peyton Place," and she and John had met on the set of the made-for-TV movie, *The Boy in the Plastic Bubble*. Diana had undergone a mastectomy some years before, and for a while, they thought she had made it.

But in March, 1977, in the middle of filming, John went back to California to be with her, and on March 27, she died. For the memorial service, John wore the white suit he and Diane had bought together for their planned trip to Rio after *Fever* was finished. It was, he says, the hardest ten weeks of his life. His director says that some of the finest parts of the movie were filmed during that time.

Saturday Night Fever will be blazing on movie screens in this country for months to come, and it is just beginning to spread the disco dancing mania to Europe. But John Travolta has no intention of remaining Tony Manero.

"I don't want my career to be over tomorrow," he says, "and I don't want to be typed. There was a potential of making an exorbitant amount of money, like $25,000 for personal appearances, just to go on and sign autographs. The smartest thing I did was not to do that."

At a restaurant table during an interview, he demonstrated with two tea cups and a cruet of soy sauce just what kind of a professional lies behind this face of Tony Manero.

He took a teacup in each hand. "My route was to go from here to there as an actor," he said, and slid the cup in his left hand across the tablecloth to the cup in his right hand.

"*This* showed up from nowhere," he continued, tilting the cruet which represented pop fame and teen worship. "I looked at it and went right on the way I was going. So you see, I never once went with something I hadn't planned on."

Does he ever wonder about the real Tony Maneros?

"They—he, Tony—wants something more out of life than his surroundings offer him. He knows he has the potential to go ahead, but he doesn't know how."

John Travolta thought a moment. Then, "I think he has a fear that his life is crumbling."

Jeff Zinn

"I spent my wedding night with John Travolta," kids Jeff Zinn, "and you can print that."

Jeff is the young New York actor who served as John Travolta's stand-in during the New York City filming of *Satur-*

Travolta doing his stuff at premiere of *Saturday Night Fever*
WIDE WORLD PHOTO

day Night Fever. He was married while the film was still shooting, and took the subway directly from the ceremony to that night's location.

A serious actor, Jeff worked days on *Saturday Night Fever* and returned to Greenwich Village every night, where he was appearing in an off-Broadway production. At twenty-seven, he has few ambitions about becoming a star but is very serious about becoming an actor.

"Being around John gave me a sense of what it would be like to be a star," he says, "but I would rather be someone who works all the time without being mobbed when I walk down the street."

He was "mobbed" more or less regularly every day after the shooting ended and he left the set. Being Travolta's stand-in had given him a measure of sudden celebrity status. The girls who collected at every location would hang around, waiting for Travolta.

"I think I became a sort of surrogate star for them," says Jeff. He signed his sought-for autograph: "To be saved in case of stardom. Love, Jeff Zinn."

Karen Gorney

From Queen of Soap to Queen of Disco was quite a character leap for Karen Gorney, known and loved by millions of television viewers across the country as "Tara" in the soap opera, "All My Children."

As Tara, the role which she originated, she was the one sweet and reliable character of the show, and so popular that no one—her producers or her audience—would let her change.

"She is one of the last vestiges of a pre-Women's Lib woman," says Karen, and the total opposite of Stephanie, the character she plays in *Saturday Night Fever*. It is Stephanie, the Brooklyn girl who has escaped to Manhattan, who becomes Tony's dance partner, who helps him to grow up, and who gives him a direction in which to move.

"Tara will be forced to stay in Pine Valley forever," says Karen, "but Stephanie is already on her way."

Born in Hollywood, Gorney is now a New Yorker, living on the West Side where she pursues her career as an actress, a singer, and a painter. She comes from a theater family. Her father is the producer-composer Jay Gorney, known in California as the man who discovered Shirley Temple, and credited with more than 300 songs—including the famous Depression anthem, "Brother, Can You Spare a Dime?" Her mother, Sondra, is a director-writer who has also worked with the Dramatic Workshop of the New School in New York, and with the American Theater Wing.

Karen attended New York's High School of Performing Arts, studied at the Carnegie Institute of Technology and at Brandeis University, where she achieved a Master of Fine Arts degree in theater. As a contemporary young woman, she identifies much more with Stephanie than she does with Tara.

"As far as survival is concerned," she says, "Stephanie is

much tougher than Tara." Tara really wasn't all that tough—despite the fact that in the course of her television life she has had to deal with family feuds, fatal diseases, ill-timed pregnancies, and a sweetheart called away to war duty.

For those who wonder what happened "after" the movie ended, Karen is willing to stick her neck out with a prediction:

"I see Stephanie working her way up and becoming a top agent and eventually a producer. She's a street kid determined to make it, and she will. As for Tony, he'll have a tough time keeping up with her, but I think they'll be tight for a long time to come."

Donna Pescow

It took her two years to get rid of her Brooklyn accent. Then, in her first film role, Donna Pescow had to "get it back" again.

Donna is the young Brooklyn-born actress who plays Annette, the girl who worships Tony Manero in *Saturday Night Fever*, and whom he leaves behind in Bay Ridge at the story's end.

Donna understands Annette well. "All she wants is a home, a husband, and a family. That's all she's seen. She works at attracting Tony, and everything is for him. And I understand women like that."

The five-foot-one, green-eyed actress began her career when she was named "Miss Sing" of Sheepshead Bay High School. "I couldn't imagine anything better happening!" Later she studied at the American Academy of Dramatic Arts, and then toured with a company of *Ah! Wilderness* with Richard Kiley and Barbara Bel Geddes.

"After that, I became queen of the callbacks for a while. But it's all worked out for the best. Those people who said they would remember me actually did." One of those callbacks led to an audition for a part in *Saturday Night Fever*.

In the interim, however, she had done a stint on a daytime soap opera, "One Life to Live," had been the "warm and creamy" girl in a department store, engraved Christmas ornaments with a gyrating machine, but "thank goodness, had the sense to turn down a job hopping around on a pogo stick announcing the opening of a bank."

"Usually I've played the girl-next-door who gets the guy," she says of her experience with the character of Annette, "but I like roles that let you stretch. It could be Pollyanna or a hooker. I don't care who I play if the part clicks. Roles that are challenging are the most fun."

That could explain her great admiration for Bette Davis whom she describes as "one of the finest actresses, period; because she can do anything at all. She's a strong lady and I admire her both personally and professionally."

Annette of Brooklyn's Bay Ridge may have been a loser, but Donna Pescow's moving portrayal may have opened the doors to a long and bright career as a fine, serious actress.

Like Bette Davis, perhaps.

★★

One of the biggest discotheques in the world was only a disco for a night. Robert Stigwood, producer of *Saturday Night Fever*, invited 800 people to dance in the "world's largest disco," an 18,000-square-foot dance floor constructed especially for him at Paramount Studios. The occasion was a bash to follow the Hollywood premiere of the Travolta film. The cost: $150,000—enough to build a pretty nice *permanent* disco.

Later that week, Stigwood paid another $75,000 to have Steve Rubell and Ian Schraeger of Studio 54 turn Central Park's famous Tavern on the Green into a disco for one night only—for a party following the premiere of *Fever* in New York City.

★★

Once Upon a Time

It all began, the myth-makers tell us, back in France in the 1950s, in some sleazy waterfront bar in Marseilles. French sailors had brought back with them the latest, hard-to-find records from the United States, put them on a phonograph, and danced the night away. And then one day they sailed away, as sailors do, leaving behind not only the girls, but those American records, too, to be stored in a sort of revolving library.

And thus was established the *discotheque*—a "place for records," literally, or a "record library"—and eventually, a place to dance to records in a record library.

Or, to put it simply, a disco.

Before long, the idea of a library of music spread to Paris where a club called Chez Castel took the sailors' idea, added chic, and sent the new thing on to London, from whence it found its way to the United States. That return wave hit the shores of the United States—New York, particularly—in the late sixties.

In those early discos in New York, such as Oleg Cassini's Le Club, or L'Interdit in the cellar of the Gotham Hotel, disco dancers could spin themselves silly to the sound of recorded music.

Then came Arthur (or, as the really "in" folk pronounced it, Arfer), New York's first chic disco, opened on the East Side of Manhattan in 1965 by Sybil Burton, the silver-haired Welsh woman Richard Burton had left for Elizabeth Taylor. Arthur established itself almost at once as the trendy new shrine of chic. It was so in, in fact, that you needed a connection to *get* in. Even Rock Hudson was once turned away by the husky fellows at the door.

The roster of regulars at Arthur was pure, unadulterated

core. These were the glamour-people, the names, the celebrities and so-called Beautiful People, the trend-setters and the trend-followers who drifted from disco to disco as one got boring or a new and more exciting one opened. Some of the names and faces on that core-list of nearly thirteen years ago at Arthur can be found in New York New York and Studio 54 today: Leonard Bernstein, Lauren Bacall, Rudolf Nureyev, Truman Capote, and the wife of the Republican Senator from New York, Marion Javits.

Arthur had replaced the Peppermint Lounge (of Twist fame) as the place to go—and, in fact, the Lounge had replaced the Stork Club. Arthur gave birth to Le Jardin, a midtown cavern of sound and light, a steamy, dreamy setting built by John Addison in the basement of the old welfare hotel, The Diplomat.

(Le Jardin is gone, today, but just next door, last June, in the old Henry Miller Theater, a new discotheque called Xenon arrived, hopefully to give Studio 54 a run for its trendy money.)

Le Jardin was bigger, wilder, and immediately more "in" than anything that had gone before, and overnight, discos started popping up all over town. But—with a few tasteful exceptions like Le Club, Le Jardin, Hippopotamus, and Shepheard's—those early discos of the sixties were tacky little boîtes, bare-wall closets wired for din and push and crush. In most of them, the sound systems were poor, the rooms small, and dancing resembled a shoving match. By the end of the sixties, most discos were considered passé.

At the same time came the rise of rock stars and the phenomenon of the mass rock concerts and mind-bending drugs that let people dance in their heads rather than on their feet. When the rock concert hall—indoor and out—took the place of the ballroom at the end of the sixties, dancing stopped. And it didn't start again until rock stars began to age and rock music began to die, until Vietnam was finally over and protest and revolt were no longer needed, until recession and economic squeeze set in.

And people started looking around for something cheaper and more fun to do.

The discotheque, with its inexpensive music, had never really disappeared from the city's black and Latin neighborhoods, or from the gay communities, all of them minorities who couldn't get into most of the chic clubs anyway. And just when those who know such things had decided that the disco bubble had burst, along came Regine with her own ideas about what a discotheque should be—and New York City went crazy again.

Mammoth clubs like Infinity, Les Mouches, and 12 West opened their doors down in Greenwich Village and in waterfront warehouses. Class clubs like Hippopotamus II and Le Club were joined by Sybil's and Doubles and LaFolie. Then came Studio 54, extravagant, exciting, theatrical, and the immediate focus for every press photographer and all the paparazzi in town. The media love affair with Studio 54 made disco an international fascination and spurred the spread of discotheques from east to west.

And then came *Saturday Night Fever* and worldwide discomania.

The discotheque, it seems safe to say, is here to stay.

Dance Fever

Discomania is not the first wave of dance fever to sweep the world. In the Middle Ages, people driven to mass anxiety by the Black Plague tried to shake off their worries in a "dancing madness."

In 1374, in Aachen, Germany, frenzied mass dancing in the streets left scores of persons in assorted states of injury and exhaustion. The outbreak followed the feast of St. John the Baptist, which was always accompanied by public dancing.

Another wave of dancing madness that swept the European continent during the Middle Ages was blamed on mildew in the rye crop.

Throughout the 1400s, in London, hordes of people would suddenly begin to dance feverishly in the streets for as long as five days at a time, until they fell from exhaustion.

In the 1800s, a new dance called the waltz captured dancing feet on both sides of the Atlantic, and "a waltz, a waltz, another waltz" became the battle cry of the ballroom.

In the early 1900s, ragtime, introduced to the world by Irving Berlin's "Alexander's Ragtime Band," swept both continents, producing the Turkey Trot and other similar dances that fitted the new and exciting "ragged time."

A wave of dance fever with the Latin touch was generated in 1912 with the introduction of the tango, and "tango teas" became the rage, while young men slicked their hair and drooped their eyelids in an effort to look like Valentino.

In the 1920s, dance madness took the form of the Charleston, the Black Bottom, and similar hyper goings-on symptomatic of the years before the stock market crash.

During the early 1930s, dance marathons plagued the United States (they were prohibited in European dance halls), and shuffling couples from coast to coast "entertained" watchers, until the government finally put a stop to the whole thing. The earliest victim of that lunacy was one Homer Morehouse, twenty-seven, of North Tonawanda, New York, who, in 1923, in order to win a bet, whirled around to the muffled strains of a country club band for 87 hours. Then, leading his exhausted partner off the floor, he fell in a heap and died.

The last great wave of dancing fever occurred during those Depression years when dancing was a recreation available to all, rich or poor—and most were poor. In dance halls like Roseland in New York, and the Aragon and Trianon in Chicago, people could forget hard times for a while.

And now, it's the Hustle—and discomania—and Saturday Night Fever at home and abroad.

Hard times are a major contributor to this current wave, too, say some authorities. The greatest interest in dancing is among those in their late teens and early twenties—the age where energy is highest and funds for recreation the tightest. But older couples are also dancing again. "Their blue-chip stocks have dipped," says one expert. "They're looking for cheaper diversions."

Disco and the economic crunch may be closing the generation gap.

Sour Notes in the Ballroom

Virtually every new dance craze—since and with the exception of the minuet—has had its critics.

The Waltz: Introduced in the early 1800s, it shocked the proper because of the embracing position of the partners. The idea of a man dancing with his hand upon a lady's waist was unthinkable, and it was viewed as a wicked dance—and banned by the Church in Germany.

The Turkey Trot: It was banned in Boston (along with the Bunny Hug, the Grizzly Bear, and every other ragtime dance) by the Mayor of Boston, John "Honey Fitz" Fitzgerald, grandfather of President John F. Kennedy.

The Tango: It swept the country in 1912, and in 1915, the Reverend Billy Sunday denounced it as "the most hellish institution that ever wriggled from the depths of perdition."

The Fox Trot: One of the early ragtime dances, it was described as "absolutely indecent. Suffice it to say that there are certain houses appropriate for such dances; but such houses have been closed by law."

The Charleston: In the 1920s, the United Dancing Masters of America debated that this wicked step was "too vulgar to deserve official recognition."

The Big Apple: A dance of the 1930s, it came out of an obscure black nightclub in Columbia, South Carolina, and critics complained that it "combined all the worst elements of the Charleston, the Black Bottom, Trucking, Shag—and the Virginia Reel!"

The Lindy/Jitterbug: Originating in the American South, the dance swept the country but was viewed with alarm because it was "preferred by groups whose main objective is the enjoyment of expressional orgies." During the early years of World War II, it was considered unpatriotic because it was the favorite dance of kids in zoot suits—and zoot suits used up scarce fabric needed by the armed forces.

The Twist (and the Frug and all the related frenetics of the 1960s) was blasted by no less than President Dwight D. Eisenhower as being "on a par with the vulgarity, sensuality and, indeed, downright filth" he saw in books and magazines and movies.

Ike yearned publicly for the minuet.

12

At the Discotheque

For those readers who have never been to a discotheque—and for those disco enthusiasts who are always looking for new and interesting clubs to visit—we have prepared a disco trip to take you inside some discotheques in this country and abroad.*
In the following pages, you will find a list of discos, compiled, researched, and drawn from many sources, and as accurate as possible a reflection of the disco action.

Some readers will recognize that many of the discotheques listed are gay discos or gay clubs. *Billboard* magazine has estimated that at least 50 percent of the discotheques in the country are gay, which is not surprising since the disco movement got its primary impetus from the gay community. Invariably, as news about a new gay club with great sound and decor gets around, straight people who want to dance start knocking at the door. A number of gay discos have opened their doors to straight people, and most of the cosmopolitan discotheques invite gay men to become members because they are enthusiastic dancers, knowledgeable about music, and add to the excitement of the disco mix.

Many discotheques are private membership clubs and are just as hard to get into as an exclusive country club. Others are membership clubs that are affordable by a wider range of people and open their doors to nonmembers when there is room. Still others are public disco dance halls where you pay your money and go in and dance.

The best rule to follow when trying out any new discotheque: "When in doubt, phone first."

Note: The tour is arranged alphabetically by city, and the discos are arranged alphabetically within each city.

Atlanta, Georgia

The Casbah: A harem-style disco that stays open until eight in the morning and helps its customers recover from a night of dancing by serving hearty breakfasts. It's *the* place to be in Atlanta these days.

Penrod's: A lushly decorated, laid-back environment, in a town where the disco scene is as hot and trendy as it is in New York. Penrod's is one of the newest and swingingest of the city's hotspots.

Other Hot Discos: *Burt's Joint*; *Fox Hunt*; *Harrison's*; *Smuggler's Inn*

Boston, Massachusetts
Boston Boston
The Fan Club
15 Lansdowne

Chicago, Illinois

Faces: A private disco on Chicago's Near North Side, where a sophisticated urban crowd listens to music through a $45,000 sound system and dances on a raised floor of computerized flashing lights, while fog envelops them to the knees. Lights are designed to program the dancers' moods—red to create intimacy, blue for coolness, and green that says "go" to aggression. Celebrity guests have included Joe Namath, Robert Conrad, Evel Knievel, Joey Bishop, Tom Jones. Faces sponsors an annual charity event each year, hosting a dance marathon to benefit children's charities. Membership costs $300 a year.

Other Hot Discos: *BBC*; *Dingbat's*

The scene at New York New York sums up the appeal of disco
PHOTO AND LIGHTING BY DESIGN CIRCUIT, INC.

Harrisburg, Pennsylvania

Class I: A New York-style disco where the dress code caters to flash city. The owner describes the atmosphere as a place to dance and party and drink. Patrons range in age mostly between twenty-one and thirty-five, but older people enjoy the place, too. Dancing is almost entirely free-style, and decor is seventies-disco with mirrored walls and neon lightning bolts. The light show changes every two weeks. The regulars are fashionable, progressive, style-conscious. Cover charge is $2.

Other Hot Discos: *Rumplestiltskin's*; *Wonderful Wanda's*; *Warehouse*

Houston, Texas

élan (with a lower-case "e") claimed 6,000 members after only six weeks in business. Membership is $200 a year.

Pistachio's: A dance floor that vibrates with changing lights and sounds, and a decor that is Art Deco–New York with silver, glass, leather and brass, and mirrors, mirrors, mirrors. The dance floor is the center for a dazzling audiovisual show produced by sixteen computer-controlled projectors that spew an endless array of images on the floor—you'll see fire and snow and Tiffany diamonds—and Farrah Fawcett-Majors. The music is loud and avant-garde and geared to dancing, not listening. Club membership is $100 a year, but nonmembers interested in joining can see it free by getting a patron card at the door. The happy hour, featuring three-for-one drinks, is open to the public.

Other Hot Discos: *Annabelle's*; *Ciao*; *The Crazy Banana*; *Mirage*

Jacksonville, Florida

Zachary's: Designed by GLI and Digital Lighting, this discotheque features a glittering disco floor and a low-key European style lounge. The environment includes a two-story waterfall, a natural rock cascade, a thousand feet of mirrors, hanging plants, an aquarium with room for more than 500 tropical fish. The largest mirror ball in the state of Florida hangs over the 700-square-foot dance floor which is lit with flashing, crashing, and spinning light strips.

Kelso, Washington

Catch a Rising Star: Owned and operated by Bo and Terry Brusco, who were on board the ill-fated Pan Am jumbo jet that collided with a KLM 747 in the worst air crash in commercial aviation. The Bruscos had been touring European discotheques, researching ambiance and ideas—and the result of their research is a discotheque that has the sound and light ambiance of a New York club, with the comfort and relaxed atmosphere of European disco rooms. There are mirrors on two walls and on the ceiling over the main dance floor, which produces a kaleidoscopic effect of multicolored lights. A sixteen-armed starburst on the ceiling, a rainbow strobe system, and tube lights grooved into the steps leading up to the main dance floor produce a spacy yet comfortable atmosphere. The general admission room is geared to young adults. Dress is casually elegant.

Key West, Florida
The Monster

Los Angeles, California

Dillon's in Westwood Village is located in a former carpet warehouse and boasts four floors—one loud. On each floor, patrons can monitor the action elsewhere in the disco on closed-circuit TV. Appearing on the floor—and the screens—are the likes of Barbra Streisand, Elton John, Lindsay Wagner, and Shaun Cassidy who drive down when they're in town.

Dillon's Downtown is a second unit which features the nightly entrance of the deejay who flies to his booth in a smoky explosion on stage (by way of rigging designed especially for flying deejays).

Studio One, formerly the Factory, will be five years old in January, 1979, and features the best disco sound around. A super disco with a football-field size floor, gays, women and straight men all go there.

Other Hot Discos: *Checkers*; *Sergio's Le Club*

Miami, Florida
The Cricket
Limelight (Hollywood, Florida)
Swinger's Lounge (Hollywood, Florida)

Minneapolis–St. Paul, Minnesota
Maximillian's
Scattie on Seventh
Smuggler's Inn
Sutton's

New Orleans, Louisiana

Georgie Porgie's Restaurant and Discotheque: Jammed to the rafters—if there were any rafters. This is a great couples and singles scene located in the Poydras Plaza (street-level floor) of the Hyatt Regency Hotel. Stained glass, a long bar, chic young people. Fun.

The Rainforest: Atop the thirtieth floor of the New Orleans Hilton Hotel and Towers, this beautiful disco is equipped with Juliana's sound system, attractive young women deejays, and a magnificent view of the Mississippi River far below. You'll be surrounded by gnarled cypress trees, and in the course of the dancing, tropical thunderstorms burst, thunder thunders, and rain pours. A floor mist and a burst of bubbles from the ceiling are a part of the fun here.

Other Hot Discos: *Cisco's*; *Fat City*; *Fletcher's Nightery*; *Le Bistro*; *The Parade*

Newport Center, California

Picassios: In Newport Beach, where you line up on Friday and Saturday nights and wait an hour to get into the popular spot, to enjoy its 140-foot-long bar, light show, sophisticated sound system. There are closed-circuit TV sets around the room where you can watch the dancers or watch special films; a backgammon room with weekend tournaments. Some 12,000 to 13,000 people throng to the place in the course of a week—most of them between twenty-five and forty, and most of them professionals, upper-echelon secretaries, and office workers.

New York City

La Folie: 21 East 61st Street. An after-hours disco. Before or during hours, it's a zany place where you'll see a couple of dozen men's and women's feet sticking out from under the bar, which has lucite stools and serves champagne and caviar during the happy hour. The dance floor is an inlaid marble roulette board, and in the ladies room long-lashed eyes stare up from porcelain toilet bowls with lucite seats. In the men's room (we're told), you can sit in a giant silver hand and make phone calls. In the ceilings, multicolored snowflake patterns are multiplied to infinity. There are marbled floors and mirrors and paintings and walls of green malachite.

Les Mouches: 260 11th Avenue. In a warehouse district near the Hudson River, this is one of the most danceable discos you'll find. It attracts a mixed crowd of gays and straights with its beautiful lighting and a great expanse of dance floor which is crowded enough to be exciting, yet open enough to let you move. There is a terrific deejay and a surround of sound that keeps you dancing hours after you'd decided to quit. If you have dinner in the Continental restaurant, there's no additional charge for dancing. One could wish Les Mouches were a little more accessible—especially to taxicabs at three o'clock on a cold winter morning. But the staff are very disposed to help you get transportation home—and there are radio cabs to be summoned. This discotheque is marked by a tasteful decor, a feeling of spaciousness, and a high level of energy and excitement. There are cabaret nights and movie nights and special theme parties at Les Mouches. It's a good idea to call in advance. In any case, reservations are a must.

Other Hot Discos: *Barbizon Plaza Library*; *Cachaça*; *Copa Disco*; *Hurrah*; *Ice Palace*; *Le Club*; *Les Nuages*; *Levitticus*; *One's*; *Reflections*; *Roseland Ballroom*; *Starship Discovery*; *Sybil's*; *Twelve West*

New York–Long Island:
Blue Cloud; *Club Marakesh*

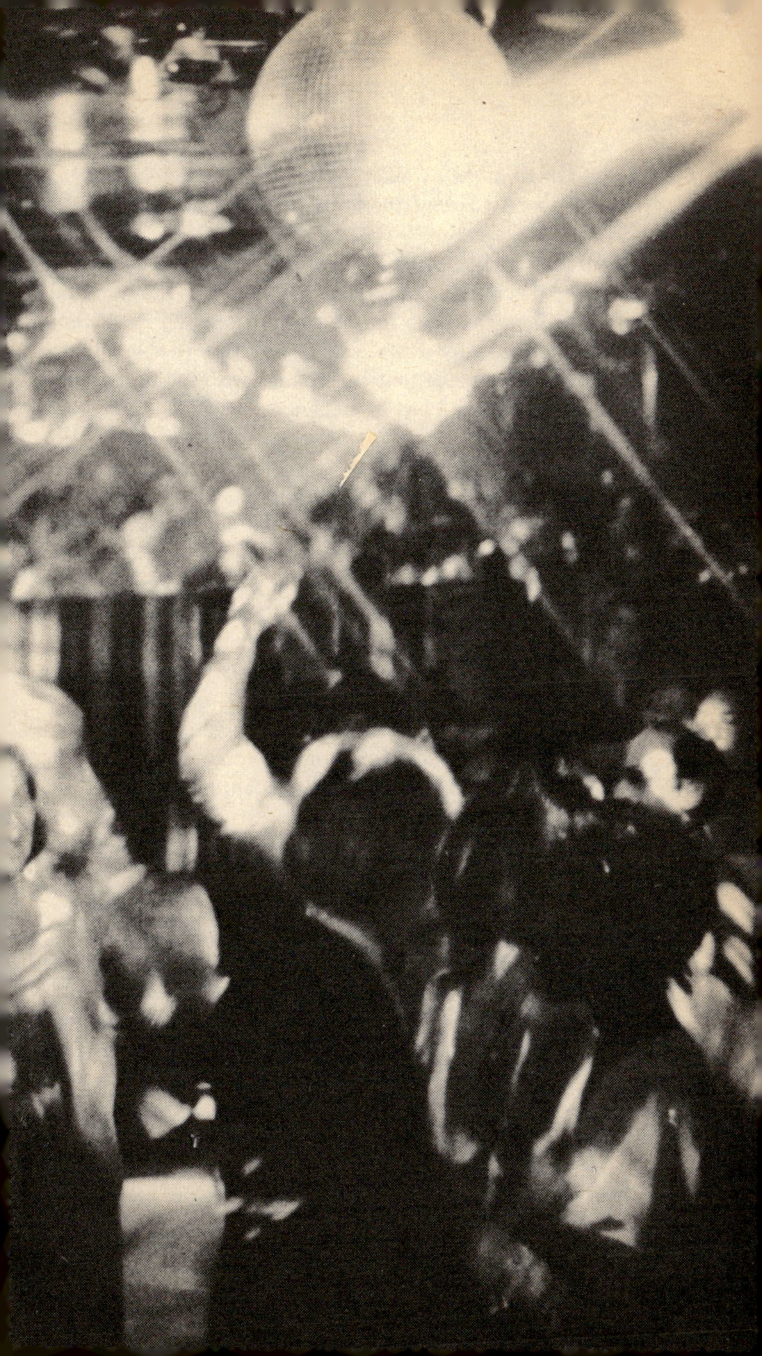

Paris

Castel's: Arabian money spoken here. Very very high society. Very expensive. Also very fine food and exquisite service.

Le Palace: Called the Studio 54 of Paris, it attracts the international set such as Paloma Picasso, Yves St. Laurent and friends. Le Palace has been in one form or another of the entertainment business for forty years, and this four-level fun house is obviously a place that can change with the times. The style is rococo, with touches of elegance.

New Jimmy's: This small, dimly lit boîte on the Boulevard Montparnasse, opened by Regine more than sixteen years ago, was a smash hit then and is a favorite today for late, late-night dancing. (No one shows up before midnight.) The clientele is second-generation New Jimmy's, and they come in couples or groups, wearing everything from jeans to blazers, and ascots to dresses. The place really gets going about 2 A.M., and the dancing goes on until 5 or 6 A.M. If Regine herself is in town, those who last that late—or early—may be treated to a spaghetti breakfast. *Note*: New Jimmy's is a private club, and in the manner of Paris private clubs, one is either known or not known at the door. Make arrangements accordingly.

Elysée Matignon: This is a kind of celebrity disco that is fairly chic, very expensive, with an expensive restaurant. Design Circuit, the wizards who did New York New York, Infinity, and the new Scaramouche, designed this disco on the Champs Elysées. The place is a three-level affair with a disco café and piano bar on the main floor, while a restaurant and special video room occupy the upper floors. Lights are reflected in mirrored walls with angled patterns, and lights chase, spin, and fill the space with undulating movement.

Photo on preceding page: The scene at New York New York sums up the appeal of disco

PHOTO AND LIGHTING BY DESIGN CIRCUIT, INC.

Regine's: Exactly like New York Regine's, very Art Deco, very expensive, very "in" to be in. It's a private club and very difficult to get into.

Club Sept: This is one of the most popular in Paris. You'll see most of the fashion designers here at one time or another.

La Ventura: A cosmopolitan spot with a very sophisticated clientele of music and film people. It cost $2 million to build, but it's hidden behind a deceptive little storefront below a coiffeur; you must descend two floors to the cellar where the disco is located.

François Premier: You'll find attractive couples here. It's very very chic and very expensive.

Florence

Jackie O's is full up here, with the very very hip and the very very young.

Davina, in Florence, caters to an older, more chic crowd, something like the Studio 54 set.

London
Annabelle's

Milan

Davina sports very much a Regine's crowd, chic, well heeled, and interested in seeing and being seen.

Nepentha

Rome

Jackie O's, in the Excelsior Hotel, is very chi-chi and very Regine's.

San Juan, Puerto Rico
Mirage

Tokyo
Castel's
The Downbeat

★★

The disco patron in the United States today, a recent study shows, is spending on the average of $3.40 per person per night. Ten years ago, it cost him 68 cents.

★★

13

I Think I'm Gonna Fall

Roller disco! It all began because the little kids were jealous of the big kids. No kidding.

These days, roller skaters are wheeling into the disco scene a mile a minute, with roller rinks from coast to coast converting old caverns into new emporiums that incorporate lighting effects and sound systems as exciting and spectacular as you will find in any discotheque in the country. And it all came about because Americans too young to get into discos where liquor is sold wanted to get in on all that disco excitement they've been hearing about from their older brothers and sisters.

And while the discotheque mania itself is just beginning to hit the Middle West and points farther on, Middle America is losing no time when it comes to making roller disco a major entertainment phenomenon.

Disco skating has become a part of the skating culture of Chicago, Philadelphia, Michigan, Ohio, trendy Los Angeles, of course, and around the town in New York. More than a hundred rinks across the country have already taken the plunge in the last two years, says Martin Lader of *Rinksider* magazine. "And all of them are making money."

The Roller Skating Rink Operators Association of America (RSROA), a trade association which has been working hard in the past ten years to upgrade the quality and image of roller skating rinks, has been conducting an almost weekly battle page in its newsletters on the pros and cons of going disco. The pros seem to be winning the argument. For when it comes to the final deciding factor, it will be what it always is in any business—the bottom line.

Maurice Johannessen, operator of a rink called California Viking Skating Country in Redding, California, wrote that he had invested $45,000 in disco sound and lighting equipment and five months later "damn near had it back already" in increased business.

Michael D'Orso, owner of the Colerain Skate Land in Cincinnati, Ohio—the biggest rink in the state with a main floor that holds 1,100 skaters—has installed all disco equipment and plans to give weekend nights to disco dancing. A hardwood maple floor that is great for skating is also great for dancing, he says.

"Several years ago," says D'Orso, "rinks were the second-class entertainment of America. Today they've been upgraded to the point where some of the new rinks may cost as much as a million dollars. I think disco will do a lot for skating, too. It's slowed the kids down a little, for one thing. Now they have dance movements for their feet—and they put their own steps together."

"It's good clean fun. There are a lot of towns in this country where kids don't have any place to go."

Howard Rheiner, of Lite Lab in New York, agrees. Manufacturers of electrical control equipment for entertainment lighting systems, Lite Lab is currently swamped with orders for disco-fying roller skating rinks all over the country.

"It's inexpensive entertainment," Rheiner points out. "Probably doesn't cost as much as a babysitter. Kids can skate from two in the afternoon to ten at night if they want to. Adults come, in, too, and it is a family environment and the parents love it to death. They can bring the kids and leave them and know they will be off the streets and well looked after."

Joseph Shevelson, vice-president for sales for the Chicago

★★

Disco skating, as it is practiced today, is described as coming from "The Xerox and Standard Oil School of Dance."

"First you copy what you see someone else doing," explains a skater, "and then you refine it to your own personality."

★★

Skate Company, says, "Rinks are where it's happening. There are growing reports from around the country about disco firms getting tapped to do bowling alleys, ski area lounges, ski slopes, resort restaurants, leisure rooms in large office complexes . . . Why not roller rinks?"

The Chicago Skate Company, which is the largest industry distributor of rink supplies, is firmly behind the disco concept and reports that more and more rinks are converting. For a 15,000-square-foot rink, it is estimated that it takes from $15,000 to $40,000 worth of equipment to create an adequate display. The trouble is, says one rink owner ruefully, that once you get started putting in equipment, you don't know where to stop.

The real push behind the move from roller rink to roller disco, is of course, people. They love it. In New York, roller rocking really got rolling at the Empire Rollerdrome in Brooklyn where the music is loud, lights flash, and hundreds of bodies in low-flying attitudes streak by at twenty miles per hour, speeded up and/or slowed down by the music.

As at any discotheque, the deejay is the man who runs the show.

"He has to know when to lay down the heat and when to cool the skaters out," said one disc jockey. "If you put on more than three fast records in a row, you won't have anyone standing. These folks will dance to what you play."

Today's new skating equipment makes dancing a lot easier than it used to be. Cryptonic wheels and laced leather boots, sealed precision ball bearings and a wide platform for balance can turn the clumsiest neighborhood kid into a wheeling Fred Astaire. And there's a large rubber ball positioned just under the toe of the skate so that you can stop on a dime.

Now, new plastic flooring developed expressly for roller skating will make it possible to design contoured paths and ramps and winding passages, so that skaters need not spend the night just going round and round. These will be an integral part of the new Rollerballroom which was to open in the fall of 1978 in Manhattan. As late as June, 1978, its founders had still not found a location—but then, they were looking for 60,000 square feet.

Judy Lynn, Bob White, and Michael Butler (producer of *Hair*) are partners in the new venture that will feature lighting by Jules Fisher (who did Studio 54 and the musical, *Dancin'*) and design by Robin Wagner, the stage designer who did the broadway show *On the Twentieth Century*.

Judy, who caught the rollerskating bug at the Empire Rollerdrome, can hardly wait to skate in her own new fantasy palace.

"Skating is now a different trip. And disco dancing on wheels is yet another different trip," she says. "So many things can happen on a moving dance floor, and you are part of it, all because you are moving rather than dancing in your own little corner.

"People can dance, moving forward, backward, while others are strutting up and through. There is no reckless speed skating—speed skating is not cool—and people rarely fall. You forget about how you look, you just get so much into moving. Liquor? You don't need it. You get so high on the energy and it's so exciting and such fun."

The word for that feeling in roller disco is "flying."

Disco Skating Tips

*Wear something comfortable. Most skaters wear blue jeans. Add a crazy hat or some other kind of disco prop if you like. It adds to the fun.

*Be sure you're wearing cotton socks. They absorb perspiration. Nylon holds the heat and it gets slippery, too.

*Don't wear glasses if you don't have to. Disco skaters are a considerate bunch, on the whole, but accidents can happen, especially to amateurs; and you don't want your 20-20s flying across the room.

*Don't be embarrassed to try because you might fall. Experienced roller disco-ers are good at scooping up topplers almost before they hit the floor. And there are usually guards and attendants around to rescue you.

*Hustle or boogie at the rail for a while, until you feel comfortable on wheels.

*Don't expect a roller disco to sound—or feel—like the 'dromes of old. The new skate wheels are polyurethane, which means they're quiet and a little soft, so that your body doesn't feel the bumps. What you hear at a roller disco is not the wheels—it's the music.

*You can buy a pair of skate boots for anywhere from $60 to a couple of hundred dollars. The expensive ones will last practically forever, so get them if you think your interest will last that long, too.

*You don't have to buy skates until you decide you really like the scene. Roller discos rent skates, and on the average the tab runs around $2 or $3.

*Don't worry about being able to dance on skates. Roller disco is like disco disco—everybody does his own thing, and everybody has a good time.

★★

Kiddie Disco

For the tens of millions of U.S. teenagers in the twilight zone when it comes to getting into fun places that serve liquor, disco entrepreneurs are creating discos-for-minors. The original Cheetah in New York City did it years ago during the first disco wave of the sixties. Ones, at 111 Hudson in New York City, has been doing it for more than a year—calling their place Disco-Tots. In Chicago, Briskman's is a 10,000-square-foot disco called Dingbats. Discotheque without liquor, a rash of boozeless discos, has also broken out in Los Angeles for those under the legal drinking age who want to party just like their older brothers and sisters.

Next: Rock-a-bye disco for the playpen crowd?

★★

Dance with Me

The dance that revived touching and brought partners back together again on the dance floor was born some time in the late sixties or early seventies. But the parentage and place of birth of the Hustle are uncertain.

Most authorities believe it came out of the Latin or Spanish-American neighborhoods of New York City.

"The Latin brothers and sisters heard the black Philadelphia sound and realized it had the same basic rhythm as salsa," says music expert Pablo Yoruba. "So they took some of the Latin stuff and added their own steps. Out came the Hustle."

Don de Natale, one of the first dancers to start teaching the Hustle back in 1973, agrees.

"Actually," he says, "no one person can invent a dance. Someone does something on a dance floor, someone else sees it and adds it to what they're doing, and eventually a dance emerges."

De Natale first saw what was to become the Hustle on Staten Island where he had been told the kids in a small club were doing an interesting new kind of dance.

"A group of us—all professional dancers—went out to see. The girls were all out there on the floor, doing these steps, and the boys were standing around the room watching—you know, the classic scene. We called the girls over and asked them what they were doing, but they couldn't really tell us, they could just *do* it.

"Finally, we broke it down into steps and then we started doing it, only we danced partners. Pretty soon, the guys around the room began to get interested, and by the time we left, some of them were out there on the floor, trying it."

The name?

Well, one version is as good as another.

Someone, watching the young people in one of the Spanish neighborhoods, asked them what it was that they were doing.

"Oh," was the reported answer, "we're jus' hustlin' around."

However it may have got its start or its name, the Hustle has played an important part in the success of the disco phenomenon.

"Every new kind of music needs a dance to keep it alive," says famed Latin bandleader Tito Puente. "With disco, it's the Hustle."

Let Yourself Go

With the birth of the Hustle, touch dancing returned to the American social scene, and discotheques, the dance halls of the seventies, exploded into a national phenomenon. And with discotheques came disco dancing—a form of dance totally divorced from the discipline of the Hustle, yet completely at home with it on the disco floor. For while the Hustle opened the way to social dancing, disco dancing has opened the pleasures of that joyous exercise to people of all ages and abilities —not just to the young, and not just to the good dancers.

Disco dancing—whether it is called free-styling or free-form—is doing-your-own-thing dancing. It is, says dancer-choreographer Peter Gennaro, what much of disco is about, and what makes it so accessible to great numbers of people. And, he emphasizes, free-styling is real dancing.

"The ability to move your body, to exercise in that way, is one way people have of expressing themselves," he says. "Professional dancers do it technically. Other people just do it. Either way, it really is dancing."

What disco dancing—free-style and otherwise—has done is make it possible for everyone to participate in one of the oldest, most pleasant of human social encounters.

If you watch for a while from the sidelines of any cosmopolitan discotheque, you'll find that no two couples are doing the same thing. Some of them may not even be moving their feet—just their bodies. But all of them are having fun. On the other hand, most of us feel more comfortable in a new experience or environment if we have at least a foggy notion of what we are supposed to be doing. In the following section, John Monte, National Dance Director of the Fred Astaire Dance Studios, has provided instructions and directions for doing some of the basic disco dancing and Hustle steps. The diagrams that accompany these instructions have been drawn by our own artists from the instructions.

We may have taken a few liberties with the language here and there, but with one or two exceptions, the instructions and steps themselves are finely honed, authentic Astaire Studio steps. Going through them at home a few times will not turn you into an Astaire, but it is certain to make you more relaxed about getting out there among all those moving bodies. Better yet, they may whet your appetite for more—and a few lessons from a trained instructor never hurt anyone.

One note for those going through these instructions:

Because disco is a trend that is moving from the East Coast to the West, the way that it is perceived and practiced differs widely from area to area. If you're a young adult, you probably know what style of disco dancing is being practiced in your area. If you're older than a young adult, ask your own teenagers or your nieces and nephews. Then pick out the steps that seem to fit your needs—and go disco.

Disco Dancing

The United States has always led the world in developing dance styles in response to their country's contemporary popular music, says John Monte. As the American composers, groups, and solo artists create ever more novel sounds, moods, and innovative rhythms, the dancing public responds to their music with ever more freedom of movement and pattern.

A new dimension in dance expression was created with the advent of the discotheques. The intimate dance floors and unusual lighting effects created an exciting and yet ultra-informal atmosphere conducive to free dance expression. No dancers ever before have been given such an opportunity to dance to such a variety of musical styles, rhythms, and arrangements.

In disco dancing almost anything goes. The dance is characterized by a casual, yet controlled, rhythmic movement of the whole body, underscored by a pulsing vertical motion through the knees. As partners dance in the "apart" position without hand-to-hand or body contact, and therefore need not lead or follow, the beat of the music may also be expressed with individual interpretations.

Steps and/or movements may be taken on each beat of the music, on each half-beat, or on each second beat of the music. The catchy throbbing beat of disco music and the do-your-own-thing nature of the dance itself give both the novice and the experienced dancer more opportunity to interpret music and rhythm personally than does any other dance. Each partner may express his individual feeling of the music by styling or rhythmic variations.

The choice of styling and intensity of body movement are up to your own personal interpretation. The following instructions should provide you with a basic framework of dance steps from which to build.

(Unless you are otherwise advised, all dance experts say your knees should always be a bit flexed—something like the position you take in golf or tennis. Bending your knees just a bit loosens your hips and leaves your body free for movement.

(At this point, remember, you're not concerned with "learning steps." What you are after is to be able to stand there and move a little bit so that you can enjoy the rhythm and the scene without feeling rooted to the ground. What you are doing in this first Fred Astaire instruction is getting the *basic disco rhythms*.

(Incidentally, perhaps we should remind you that the beat, or rhythm, of disco music is 4/4 time. You count one-two-three-four. Don't worry too much about finding the beat. The bass speakers in most discotheques are down on the floor, so you'll feel the beat in your feet (and in your rib cage, too). Totally deaf people are able to enjoy disco dancing because they can feel the beat, even if they can't hear the music.—K.H.)

A note on dance instruction terminology: We have tried to translate some of the professional language into "people language," but you should also know the correct terminology. The word "close" is a verb, as in "close the door," and it describes the action of bringing one foot to the other. The terms "point" or "touch" (which we have called "move") indicate that the foot is lifted, moved, pointed and touched lightly to the floor, but that you do not put your weight on it, and you are not taking a step. A "step" means that you move the foot and put your weight on it.

Basic Disco Rhythm

Start out by standing easily and casually, your feet just a bit apart. Since the man always starts out with his left foot, most of his weight should be on his right foot. The woman, who always starts dancing with her right foot, should feel most of her weight resting on her left foot.

Man's Steps:
1. Close your left foot to the right foot and, at the same time, flex or bend your knees slightly. — Count One
2. Now, move your right foot to the side without putting your weight on it. At the same time, straighten your knees. — Count Two
3. Bring your right foot back to the left foot and bend your knees slightly again. — Count Three
4. Now move your left foot to the side, but don't put your weight on it. Straighten the knees. — Count Four

Woman's Steps:
The woman dances the direct opposite of the man's steps, beginning with her right foot.

Now put on the music as you practice this *basic disco rhythm*. Relax and enjoy the music. You will soon feel a pulsing response to the beat. Allow your arms to swing naturally (try opening and closing—or back and forth—in coordination with the steps) and don't be afraid to turn your body a little this way and that.

Now that you've got the feet going and the arms going, try a little bit of extra styling. Lift your hip upward and to the left as you move the left foot; then lift the hip upward and to the right as you move the right foot.

Once you have practiced the *basic disco rhythm* until your body is responding to the music with an easy and comfortable motion, you can begin to do variations. Try moving your foot forward several times on the beat, and then backward. When you dance the *basic disco rhythm* moving backward, use a slight forward tilt of the body as you move the foot. When you dance the *basic disco rhythm* moving forward, try using a slight turn of the shoulders for added effect.

As you can see, we're talking about movements here rather than steps. And even though you are being taught certain movements, once you get the hang of the movements and the beat, it becomes free-styling, because it is entirely up to you which way you move and what you do with your arms and hips while you are doing it.

A Note on Diagrams: A diagram can only tell you where your foot should go, not what to do with it when it gets there. Refer to the instructions to determine whether the move is an actual *step* (with weight on it) or simply a "point" or "touch." If you have a tape recorder, you might try dictating these instructions onto a cassette and then play it back as you practice. .

Variations of the Basic Disco Rhythm

1. *Doubling Up*

Men's and Women's Steps: With the *basic disco rhythm*, you have been dancing one movement on each beat of the music. By *doubling up* the tempo, you will dance the same movements on each half beat of the music. Instead of *one, two, three, four,* you will count *and* one, *and* two, *and* three, *and* four. In this instance, you flex the knees slightly on each "*and*" count and straighten them on the counts of *one, two, three, four*. Practice the basic *disco rhythm* steps to the doubling-up count, increasing the tempo of your movements to fit the count of *and* one, *and* two, *and* three, *and* four.

2. Side Cross Step

Man's Steps:
1. Left foot steps to the side. — Count One
2. Right foot crosses in front of the left. — Count Two
3. Left foot steps to the side again. — Count Three
4. Right foot points to the side without putting your weight on it. — Count Four
5-8. Repeat the above steps, but this time beginning with the right foot to the side, and alternating the movements to the other side. — Count One, Two, Three, Four

Woman's Steps:
The woman dances directly opposite the man's steps, beginning with her right foot.

Note: As you start to dance the *side cross step* with ease, you will find that you are naturally turning slightly to the left as you move right, and turning slightly to the right as you move toward the left.

SIDE CROSS STEP

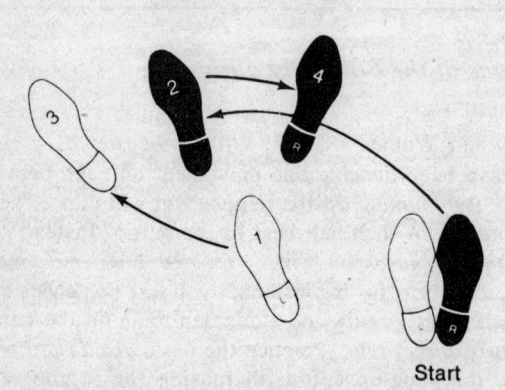

Start

3. The Bump

You will have fun dancing the *bump*, especially with a responsive partner. The basic movement of the *bump* is easy to learn. As you dance the steps described below, simply exaggerate that outward lifting of the hip where indicated. Make this a sharp motion, as if bumping an object out of your way. (Pretend you're trying to open a kitchen door with both arms filled with grocery bags.)

In the *basic disco rhythm*, you were dancing "step-move." Now that action will become "step-bump." Relax the knees so that you achieve a more fluid change of hip movement and weight. You probably will find it more fun to do several bump actions in succession.

*Note: You may also step forward on the right foot, turning one quarter to the right, followed by three *bumps*; and then step backward on the left foot, turning left before repeating the *bumps*.

You can vary the *bump* even further by replacing the forward and backward steps with a slight springing action with the feet together, and then only one *bump* lightly hitting your partner's extended hip.

Numerous other variations of the bump can be danced with your own individual interpretations. Try experimenting . . . but remember, don't bump too hard, especially if you are dancing the variations where both partners bump each other's hips. (You don't want to go home black-and-blue.)

As you can see from this small sampling of the *basic disco rhythm* and other variations, disco dancing can be great fun. When you practice, allow yourself to relax and enjoy the excitement of the music. You will soon begin to develop your own personal style with interpretive arm, body, and head movements. Don't be afraid to try varying your rhythm to the music. You are entirely on your own, and no rules apply.

Almost all the dance experts we talked to make this point: suit the movement to your own style and personality. What looks cute and sexy when a slim young thing does it can look crude and vulgar when an older person performs the same movement to the same degree. Do it, by all means, do it. But don't *over*do it.

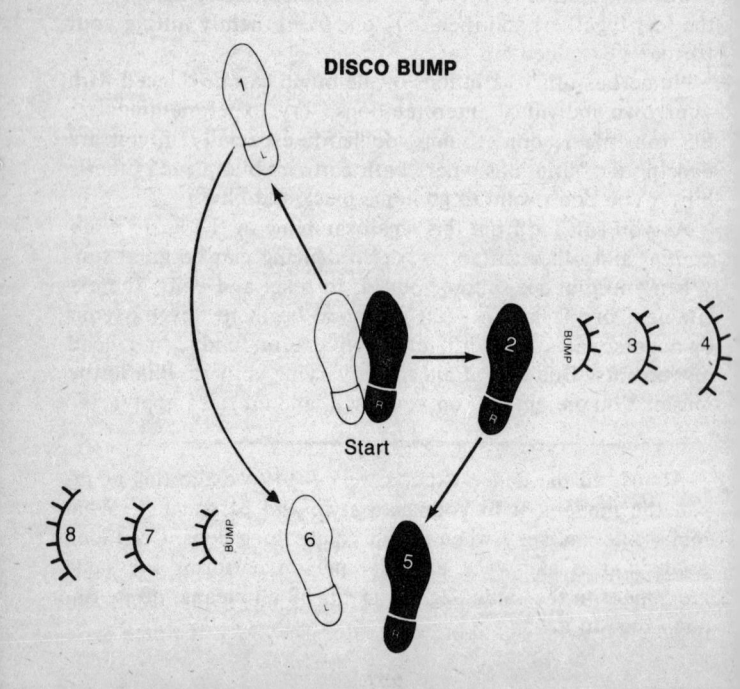

Man's and Woman's Steps:
1. Put your left foot forward, turning it a quarter (¼) to the left. — Count One
2. Right foot moves to the side, without weight; at the same time, *bump* the right hip to the side. — Count Two
3-4. Bump the right hip to the side two additional times. — Count Three, Four
5. Right foot steps backward, turning a quarter to the right. — Count One
6. Left foot moves to the side, without weight, and at the same time, bump the left hip to the side. — Count Two
7-8. *Bump* the left hip to the side two additional times. — Count Three, Four

DISCO BUMP

The Hustle

The Hustle has taken the fast, double-beat of the Swing of the forties and totally transformed the music effect by adding the arrangements and melodic interpretations of the seventies. The resulting music is upbeat, syncopated, toe-tapping—and irresistible to contemporary dancers.

The Hustle retains essentially the style and character of the contemporary disco movements, yet draws on the many variations danced in Swing by previous generations. The accepted dance position is with partners at arm's length and holding hands. This double hand-hold provides the partners with a strong contact which allows them to achieve a "push-pull" resistance which is necessary for some of the advanced steps and turns.

We are including three versions of the Hustle as it is danced throughout the country. They are: (1) the American Hustle; (2) the Latin Hustle; (3) the California Hustle, which is also known as the Bus Stop (or a line dance.)

The American Hustle will introduce you to the basic movements and patterns originally developed as touch dancing returned to vogue. The Latin Hustle soon followed, with more intricate steps and rhythms, to match the bouncy, syncopated beat of the music. The California Hustle is unusual in that it is not a partnership dance, but rather a form of group expression. Here individual dancers follow a set pattern of steps in unison. (It is sometimes called a line dance.) Like any other group dance, it can be a lot of fun. We have included this well-known sequence because of its nationwide popularity with groups of all ages.

The Basic American Hustle (Author's Version)

Because there are so many versions of even a basic American Hustle, we, as amateur dancers—well, actually, *non*dancers—have presented and diagrammed the basic and turning steps we found easiest to do. They lack the high style of the Fred Astaire Studio steps, but they will get you started.

Basic Step, Man:

Stand with feet together, just slightly apart from your partner.

1. Move left foot slightly to the side, just touching the ball of your foot to the floor, but don't put any weight on it. (Some teachers call this "point," some say "touch," but in any case, that's how you do it.) — Count One
2. Close your left foot to the right foot, transferring your weight to the left foot. — Count Two
3. Touch or point or move your right foot slightly to the side, but don't put your weight on it. — Count Three
4. Close your right foot to left foot, transferring your weight to the right foot. — Count Four
5. Step in place on the left foot. — Count Five
6. Step in place on the right foot. — Count Six

BASIC AMERICAN HUSTLE
(Man)

Basic Step, Woman:
Stand with feet together, your weight over the left foot.

1. Move the ball of the right foot slightly to the side, but do not put your weight on it. — Count One
2. Close the right foot to the left foot, transferring weight to right foot. — Count Two
3. Move the left foot slightly to the side, just touching the ball of the foot to the floor, but don't put any weight on it. — Count Three
4. Close the left foot to the right foot, transferring the weight to the left foot. — Count Four
5. Step in place on the right foot. — Count Five
6. Step in place on the left foot. — Count Six

This is easiest to learn as a partner dance if you just hold hands, in what is called a four-hand-clasp. Later you can do it in the classic dance position.

In doing the basic American Hustle, which is very informal, it isn't necessary to plant your foot in any exact spot. What is important is that you get the rhythm: "Move, step; move, step." Once you've got that rhythm, you can add Hustle styling simply by lifting your hip up and out as you move.

BASIC AMERICAN HUSTLE
(Woman)

Step in Place

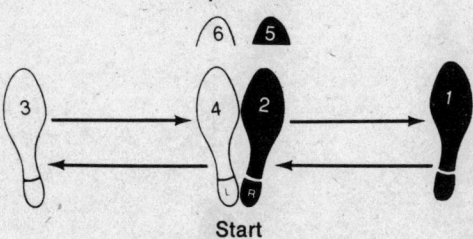

Basic Hustle Variation

This is another version of the Basic Hustle. It's a partner dance, man and woman facing each other, holding hands. The count is: one-two-three-four-five-six. The knees should be slightly bent, but not stiff.

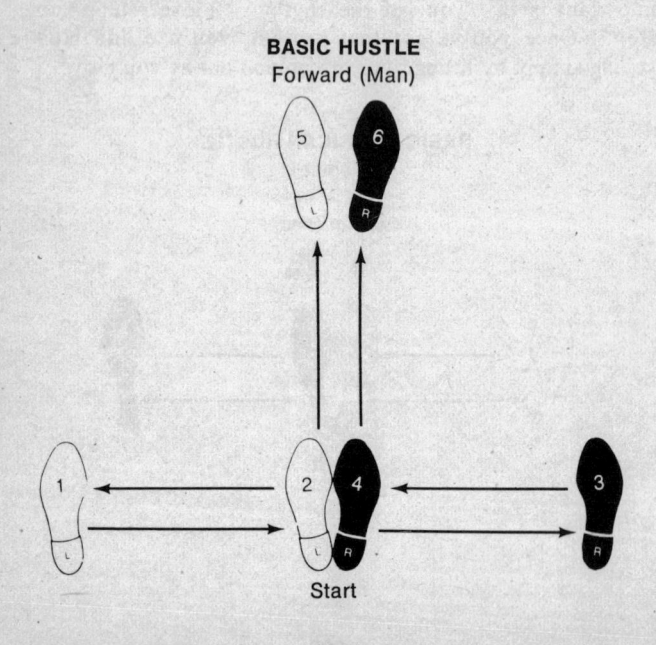

Basic Forward Steps, Man's:
1. Move the left foot slightly to the side, without putting your weight on it.   Count One
2. Bring left foot back to the right foot. Weight on left foot.   Count Two
3. Move the right foot slightly to the side, again without putting your weight on it.   Count Three
4. Bring right foot back to left foot. Weight on right foot.   Count Four
5. Step forward on the left foot.   Count Five
6. Step forward on the right foot.   Count Six.

BASIC HUSTLE
Forward (Man)

Basic Backward Steps, Man's:
1. Move the left foot slightly to the side without weight. — Count One
2. Bring the left foot to the right foot. Weight on left foot. — Count Two
3. Move the right foot slightly to the side, without weight again. — Count Three
4. Close the right foot to the left. Weight on right foot. — Count Four
5. Step back on the left foot. — Count Five
6. Step back on the right foot. — Count Six

Note: On Steps Five and Six, forward, the man pushes the woman so that she moves *backward*. On Steps Five and Six, backward, the man pulls the woman *forward*, toward him.

BASIC HUSTLE
Backward (Man)

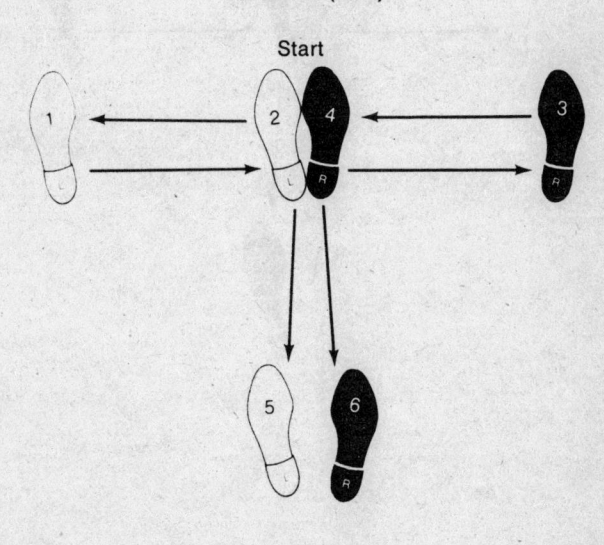

Basic Backward Steps, Woman's:
1. Move the right foot slightly to the side, no weight. — Count One
2. Close right foot to left foot. — Count Two
3. Move the left foot slightly to the side, no weight. — Count Three
4. Close the left foot to right foot. — Count Four
5. Step back on the right foot. — Count Five
6. Step back on the left foot. — Count Six

BASIC HUSTLE
Backward (Woman)

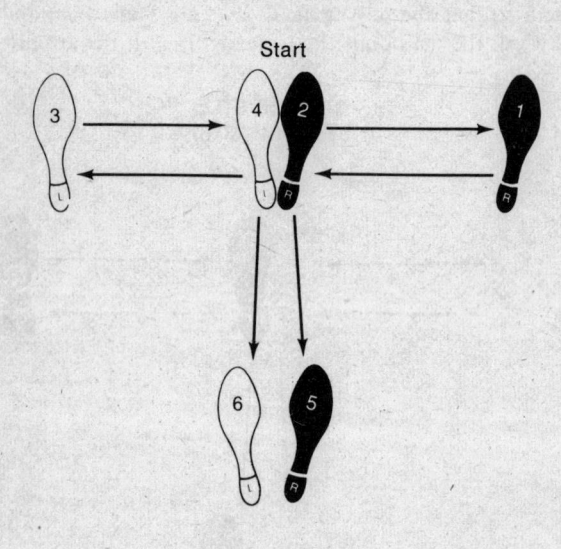

Basic Forward Steps, Woman's:
1. Move right foot slightly to one side, without weight. — Count One
2. Close right foot to left foot. — Count Two
3. Move left foot slightly to side, no weight. — Count Three
4. Close left foot to right foot. — Count Four
5. Step forward on the right foot. — Count Five
6. Step forward on the left foot. — Count Six

BASIC HUSTLE
Forward (Woman)

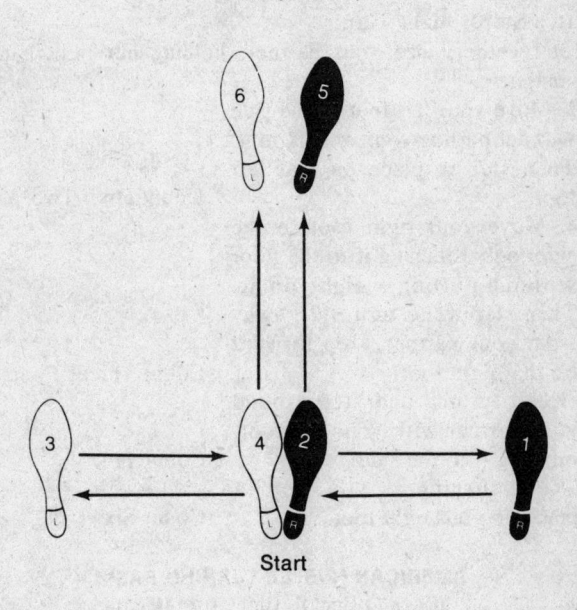

American Hustle Turning Basic

Once you have mastered the style and rhythm of the basic American Hustle, you'll find that the turning basic step (sometimes called "back to back") will give you more flexibility on the dance floor. In the following instructions notice that though you start your turn on Count Three, the *actual* turning takes place on the counts of "Four, Five, Six."

Note: "Turning" will mean that you are swiveling around on the weight-bearing foot as you bring the other one to where you want it.

Man's Steps, Right Turn:
Feet together, face your partner, holding her right hand in your left.

1-2. Move your left foot to the side without putting your weight on it. Then step in place on that left foot. Count One, Two

3-4. Move your right foot to the side, only touching it to the floor without putting weight on it. Then starting to turn *right* away from your partner, step forward on that right foot. Count Three, Four

5. Keep turning and step around your partner with your left foot, bringing it to the side. Count Five

6. Keep turning as you step in place on your right foot. Count Six

AMERICAN HUSTLE TURNING BASIC
(Back to Back) Right Turn (Man)

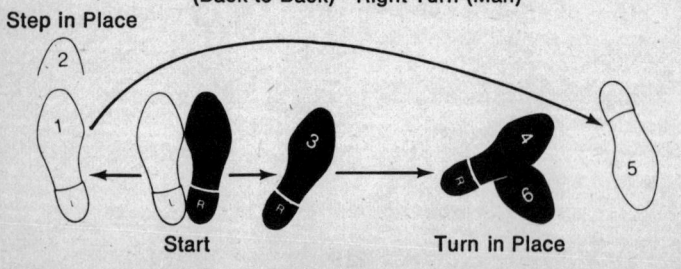

If you've done it right, the two of you should be standing back to back.

Man's Steps, Left Turn:
1. Move your left foot to the side.
2. Step in place on that left foot.   Count One, Two
3. Move your right foot to the side.
4. Starting to turn *left* toward your partner, step forward on that right foot.   Count Three, Four
5. Keep turning, step to the side on your left foot.   Count Five
6. Keep turning, step in place on your right foot.   Count Six

Now you should be facing your partner.

AMERICAN HUSTLE TURNING BASIC
(Back to Back)   Left Turn (Man)

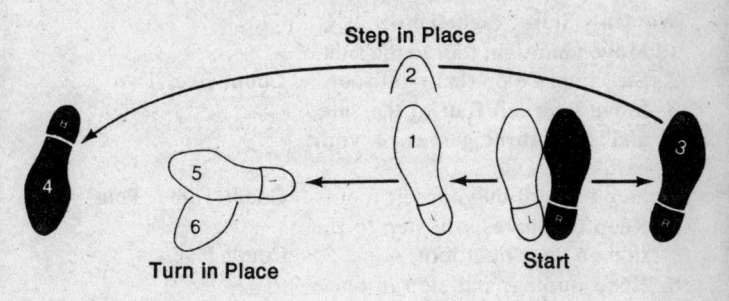

Woman's Steps, Left Turn:
Face your partner, feet together, placing your right hand in your partner's left.
1. Move your right foot to the side.
2. Step in place on your right foot.   Count One, Two
3. Move your left foot to the side and start turning *away* from your partner.
4. Step forward on your left foot.   Count Three, Four

5. Keep turning, step around to the side on your right foot.   Count Five
6. Keep turning, and step in place on your left foot.   Count Six

AMERICAN HUSTLE TURNING BASIC
(Back to Back)   Left Turn (Woman)

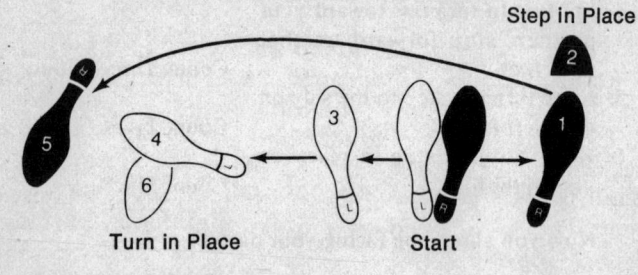

You should be standing back to back, with your right arm extended, holding your partner's hand.

Woman's Steps, Right Turn:
1. Move your right foot to the side.
2. Step in place on that right foot.   Count One, Two
3. Move your left foot to the side, and start turning *toward* your partner.
4. Step forward on your left foot.   Count Three, Four
5. Keep turning as you step to the side on your right foot.   Count Five
6. Keep turning, and step in place on your left foot.   Count Six

You should now be facing your partner.

AMERICAN HUSTLE TURNING BASIC
(Back to Back)   Right Turn (Woman)

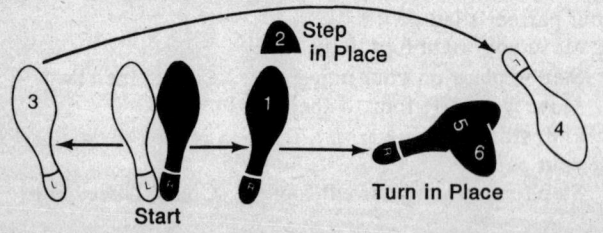

As you practice and become more adept at dancing the movements that have been described, you will find that there are a number of underarm turns that can be used.

We will describe two variations here, to give you the basic idea from which you can develop your own underarm turns. These are simply instructions that tell you how the woman is turned to move under the man's arm, either to her right or to her left.

When a man gets ready to turn his partner, he gives her a signal—simply swinging the arms upward and raising his left hand and arm while holding his partner's right hand.

The woman responds to the signal quickly and lightly, by taking her three forward steps on counts "four, five, six" in a small compact circle, moving and turning under his raised arms. To get around and under in time with the beat, you must take short, close steps.

This is the *underarm turn* with the woman turning underarm to her right.

Man's Step:

Dance the *turning basic* one time and on the counts "four, five, six" release your partner to an open position. Then take a double hand-hold and continue this way:

Dance the basic American Hustle step in an open position with a double hand-hold for the counts "one, two, three."

On count "four," swing your arms upward and raise your left hand and arm. This allows your partner to turn underarm to her right. At the same time, release your right hand-hold. The man doesn't turn—he just stands there (more or less) and lets his partner do all the work.

Woman's Step:

Dance the direct opposite of the man's steps for the *turning basic*, ending in an open position with a double hand-hold. Then continue like this:

1. Move the right foot to the side without weight.   Count One.
2. Right foot steps to the side: small step.   Count Two
3. Left foot moves to the side without weight.   Count Three

4. Left foot steps forward, starting to turn underarm to the right. Count Four
5. The right foot steps forward, continuing to turn underarm to the right. Count Five
6. Continuing to turn, left foot steps forward, completing a total of one turn underarm to the right. Count Six

This is the *underarm turn* with the woman turning to her left.

Man's and Woman's Steps:

Essentially, this variation is the same movement as the one described before, except that the woman turns in the opposite direction, underarm, to her left.

The man dances the same movements described previously, but on the count of "four," he raises his left hand and arm across the front of his body, to allow his partner to turn underarm to her left. At the same time, he lets go his right hand-hold.

The woman alters the turning direction of steps "four, five, six," so that she turns underarm to her left on those counts in a compact circle, turning under the raised arms.

The Latin Hustle

The Latin Hustle is basically an advanced and highly stylized form of the American Hustle. You give it that style by syncopating the beat between the count of "three" and the count of "four." You will count: One, two, three-and-four, five, six. This means that an additional step will be taken for each basic movement. It's the "three-and" count that gives you the extra step, which has to be done in the same space of time. The beat doesn't change. You just step a little faster to keep up with it at that point.

Man's Steps:
1. Move the left foot to the side but don't step on it. — Count One
2. Bring left foot back (close) to the right foot. — Count Two
3. The right foor steps back with a small step. — Count Three
4. The left foot closes to the right foot. — Count "and"
5. The right foot steps forward: small step. — Count Four
6. The left foot closes to the right foot. — Count Five
7. The right foot closes to the left foot (virtually a step "in place"). — Count Six

Note: These instructions and the accompanying diagram show *seven* steps or moves being taken, but the count is still Six. It's that little quickie "three-and" (which is really two moves to one beat) that makes the difference.

LATIN HUSTLE
(Man)

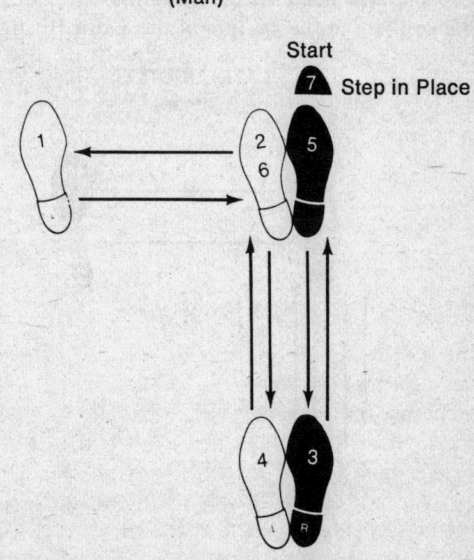

Woman's Steps:
1. Move right foot to the side, without weight on it.   Count One
2. Right foot closes to left foot.   Count Two
3. Left foot steps back: small step.   Count Three
4. Right foot closes to the left foot.   Count "and"
5. Left foot steps forward: small step.   Count Four
6. Right foot closes to the left foot.   Count Five
7. Left foot closes to the right foot. (virtually a step in place)   Count Six

*You will notice that there is a slight difference in the placement of the feet in this basic movement, as opposed to the placement of your feet in the basic American Hustle step. The difference is *the action of both partners backing away from one another on* Step Three, and then closing the feet and returning to the starting position by Step Five. This is the *primary* difference. This primary difference must be practiced carefully before you go ahead with the next variations. Once you have mastered this movement, you may want to refer back to the American Hustle variations previously described and dance them in the rhythm of the Latin Hustle.

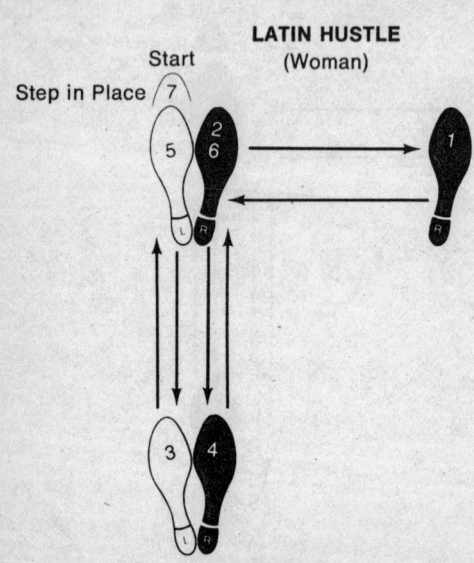

LATIN HUSTLE
(Woman)

The Latin Hustle Turning Basic Step.

Man's and Woman's Steps:

1-4. Dance Steps One through Four of the basic Latin Hustle as described before: Count One, Two, Three, "and."
5-7. Dance Steps Four through Six of the turning basic as described in the American Hustle, turning a total of one half to the right. Count Four, Five, Six.

LATIN HUSTLE TURNING BASIC (Man)

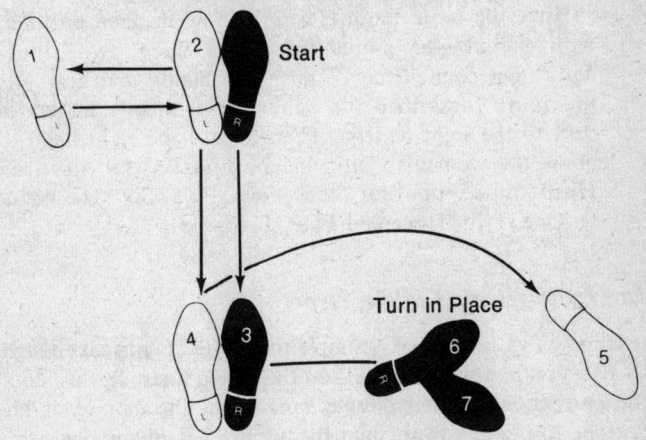

Start

Turn in Place

LATIN HUSTLE TURNING BASIC (Woman)

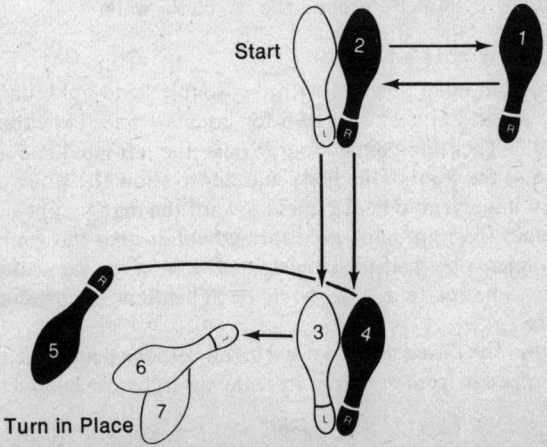

Start

Turn in Place

Underarm Turns for the Latin Hustle

Man's and Woman's Steps:

1-7. Dance Steps One through Seven of the turning basic in the Latin Hustle rhythm, releasing the woman to an open position on the counts "four, five, six." Count: One, Two, Three-and Four, Five, Six.

On "six" take a double hand-hold, then continue as follows.

8-14. Dance the basic Latin Hustle step in an open position, with a double-hand-hold for counts "one, two, three-and." On count "four," raise the hands and arms (as previously described for either the woman's underarm turn to the right or left). Then release the right hand to allow the woman to turn underarm (as in the American Hustle description) for Steps Four, Five, Six. The count is: One, Two, Three-and Four, Five, Six.

The Latin Hustle Cuddle Step

Here's a variation that is simple to do, yet is unusual enough to give you plenty of "shine" on the dance floor. In this step, the partners keep their double hand-hold. The man leads his partner to dance toward him by turning her under one arm. This brings the partners into a side-by-side position, with the man's arms "cuddled" around the woman's waist.

Man's and Woman's Steps:

1-7. From an open position with the double hand-hold, dance the basic Latin Hustle step for counts "one, two, three-and." Then, on count "four," raise the left hand and arm across the front of the body in order to allow the woman to turn underarm to her left, and toward the man's right side. Retain the right hand-hold throughout so that the woman completes her half-turn underarm facing in the same direction as her partner. She should be at his right side by count "six."

Lower the raised arms to waist level, with the man's left arm wrapped in front of his partner, and his right arm behind her in "cuddle" position. Count: One, Two, Three-and Four, Five, Six.

8-14. With the woman in "cuddle" position, dance the basic Latin Hustle step for counts "one, two, three-and four." On count "five," raise the left hand and arm to allow the woman to turn underarm to her right, so that she ends in her original starting position. The woman completes the half-turn underarm to her right on counts "five" "six." Count: One, Two, Three-and Four, Five, Six.

This small sampling of both the American and the Latin Hustle can provide a lot of fun—but be sure that when you practice, you allow yourself to relax and enjoy the excitement of the music. Take it, figuratively as well as literally, one step at a time, so that learning is fun, and so that you experience little "victories" along the way. Don't be afraid to vary your steps to the music. As long as you're in time with that 4/4 disco beat—and how could you miss it—you're all right. Before long, you will find yourself developing your own personal style in the way you move your arms, your body, and your head.

The California Hustle

This is a line dance, and a favorite among the many line dances enjoying popularity throughout the country. (Others are called the Chicago Bus Stop, the Continental Walk, the Monorail, the New Yorker, the Oasis, and, by now, there are certain to be more.) Unlike the American and the Latin Hustle, the California Hustle (also known as the Bus Stop) is danced, not as a couple, but by individuals in a group who follow a prescribed sequence of steps, in rhythm, and using the same foot. It's performed in an infinite variety of combinations in different parts of the country and even varies from town to town.

Any number can play—from two people to fifty can do the California Hustle or Bus Stop at the same time. The dancers form one or more lines across the room, the whole group faces the same direction and—if you're enjoying the action—don't worry about looking like the Rockettes in high gear. Practice the steps in a relaxed and casual manner. Since they are so simple, try to enjoy the excitement of the music while you're learning.

No distinction is made this time between the man's steps and the woman's, since they are identical. Although the dance is described here as three separate patterns, the movements are actually danced one after the other to make a complete sequence. You then repeat the sequence as often as the music requires—or as long as your legs hold out.

Back and Forward Steps:

1-3. Beginning with the right foot, take three steps backward, right, left, right.   Count One, Two, Three
4. Slap the left foot against the right foot without weight, and clap your hands.   Count Four
5-7. Beginning with the left foot, take three steps forward, left, right, left.   Count One, Two, Three
8. Slap the right foot against the left foot without weight and clap your hands.   Count Four
9-12. Repeat Steps One through Four, beginning with the right foot.   Count One, Two, Three, Four

CALIFORNIA HUSTLE (BUS STOP)
Back & Forward

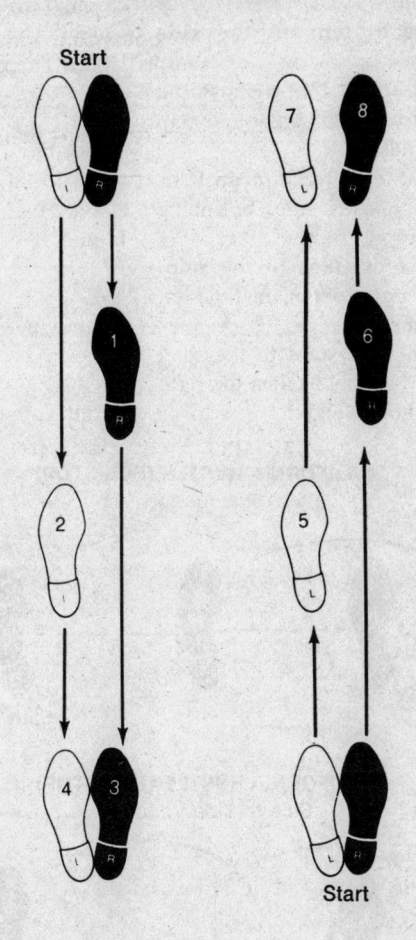

Side-to-Side Steps:
1. Left foot steps to the side.   Count One
2. Right foot crosses behind the left foot.   Count Two
3. Left foot steps to the side again.   Count Three
4. Slap the right foot against the left foot without weight and clap your hands.   Count Four
5-8. Dance Steps One through Four to the opposite side, beginning with the right foot.   Count One, Two, Three, Four
9-10. Left foot steps to the side; slap the right foot against the left foot without weight.   Count One, Two
11-22. Right foot steps to the side; slap the left foot against the right foot without weight.   Count Three, Four

CALIFORNIA HUSTLE (BUS STOP)
Side to Side

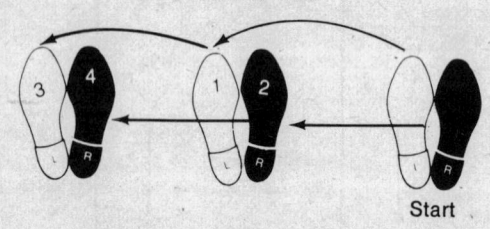

CALIFORNIA HUSTLE (BUS STOP)
Side-to-Side Variation

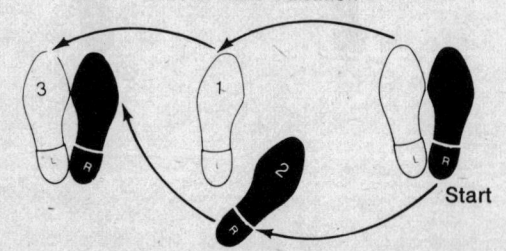

Swivel and Toe-Tap Step

The swivel and toe-tap step is the most complicated of the three patterns that make up the California Hustle. Do it slowly and carefully at first until you have become thoroughly familiar with all the movements. This is the final sequence of the California Hustle step. After you've done it, repeat all three sequences over again—and over again—starting with the back and forward steps, continuing to the side-to-side, then to the swivels and toe-taps.

Notice that your count changes emphasis on this step.

1. Swivel quickly on the balls of both feet with what might be described as a Charleston step—the heels apart and then heels together, two times. (Your feet should form a Vee-shape.) — Count "and" One, "and" Two
2. Tap the right toe forward without weight, two times. — Count Three, Four
3. Tap the right toe backward without weight, two times. — Count One, Two
4. Tap the right toe forward without weight once. — Count Three
5. Tap the right toe backward without weight once. — Count Four
6-7. Repeat Steps Four and Five once. — Count One, Two
8. Tap the right toe to the side without weight, at the same time turning one quarter to the left. — Count Three
9. Kick the right foot forward. — Count Four

Once you have learned the California Hustle (or Bus Stop), teach it to your friends. It's fun to dance at parties.

The Tango Hustle

This is done to the same basic six counts of the Hustle, but you move out almost in a straight path with your partner, your knees bent and your body low. Think of yourself as Rudolph Valentino-and-friend—slinky, sensual, and sexy.

Steps:

1-3. Start on the right foot and walk forward on Steps One, Two, Three.	Count One, Two, Three
4. Quickly bring the left toe next to the right toe. Think about stopping, but don't.	Count Four
5. Step forward on your right foot.	Count Five
6. Swivel on your right foot a bit so that you can turn and start the whole sequence over again.	Count Six

This step takes a bit of space—and considerable grace—to bring off well, but it's worth the effort.

TANGO HUSTLE

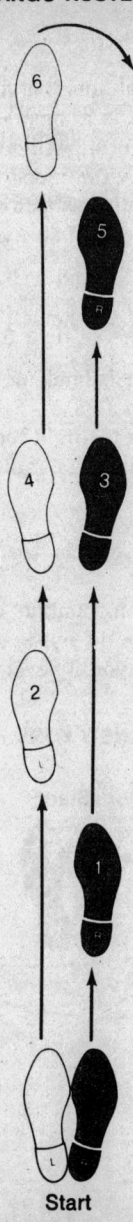

Basic "New York" Hustle

This is an easy one, although at first the diagram may look complicated. The count is a simple One, Two, Three, Four. You can do this free-form, without touching, each partner moving in whatever way the mood dictates. If you touch, of course, remember that the woman's steps are the exact opposite of the man's. The man always starts with his left foot; the woman with her right.

1. Step about 8 inches to the left and onto your left foot. — Count One
2. Bring your right foot behind the left, so that the heels form a "T." — Count Two
3. Step to the right onto the right foot. — Count Three
4. Bring left foot behind the right, so the heels form another "T." — Count Four

Repeat for four more counts—or until you feel like trying something else.

Each step takes the same amount of time.

Take small steps, since the music usually is quite fast, and if your steps are too long, you'll never make it.

BASIC NEW YORK HUSTLE

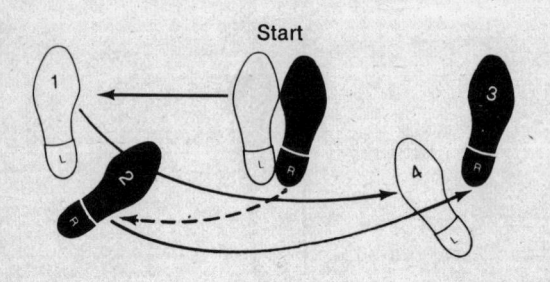

Disco Attitudes

Gettin' the Spirit

It's not a step. It's not a dance. It's an attitude. And if you can catch the attitude and keep time to music, you don't have to sit on the sidelines because you can't do the Hustle. With the right disco attitude, you can make it (or fake it) on any disco floor in the country.

The elements that will give you that disco look are not dances or dance steps, per se, but movements and positions that express an attitude. It's the way you stand, the expression on your face, the way you hold your body, your arms, that create the disco look. It's easy to learn, fun to do, and once you have the hang of it, you can stand out there on the disco floor and never move your feet—and still look as though you know what you're doing.

Following are a few hints for beginners compiled from the experience of a couple of amateurs who tried them out and found that they worked. (Remember, once you're comfortable, you can break all the rules.)

Get Ready . . .

Before you can look like anything more than a tree stump on the disco floor, you must relax.

Roll your head around from shoulder to chest to shoulder to back several times. When your neck bones stop cracking, stop.

Open and close your mouth, dropping your chin, in an imitation of a goldfish. It will relax your neck and face.

Breathe in deeply through your nose, then exhale as far and as long as you can. Feel your stomach muscles tighten. Relax. Then repeat several times.

So, Okay, Get Set . . .

*Stand up straight but don't stiffen your spine. You're not at West Point.

*Keep your chin up, unless you're bending your head to achieve a special attitude. Don't worry about your feet.

*Get your shoulders back and chest out but, again, remember you are on a dance floor, not a parade ground.

*Unlock your knees and flex them a little as though you were getting ready to take a golf swing.

*Practice in front of a mirror so that you can check your silhouette and facial expression. In the disco look, what you are doing with your eyes and mouth and eyebrows is as important as what you're doing with the rest of your body.

*Keep your arms and hands above waist level. It gives you more of an "up" feeling—and it's cooler under the arms.

Go!!!!

Now, put on a disco record and get yourself into the mood.

*Step from foot to foot in time to the music. The disco beat is 4/4 time, and what you're doing is a two-step.

*Come down on your entire foot, not just your toes. Pretend you're stomping grapes—or bugs.

*Don't feel you have to jump up and down. The ankles bend, the knees bend, the hips, shoulders, and head swivel as much or as little as you like. But you could "dance" all night and scarcely lift your feet off the floor.

*Raise your arms and hands until you look like a doctor who's just been "gloved" for surgery, moving with hands in the air toward the operating room.

*Turn your head from side to side as you move, looking down as though you see something crawling on the floor and shrugging your shoulders as though you couldn't care less.

Now look in the mirror. That's the disco look.

*Relax. Nobody's looking at you. Once you've got the look and the beat, let the music tell you what to do.

Don de Natale's Secret

The trick of really graceful-looking movement on the disco floor, say dance experts, is the simple act of shifting the weight from foot to foot. It's something we all do naturally enough when we walk, but somehow seem to forget when we get out on the dance floor. Beginners and amateurs find themselves standing on—putting all their weight on—the very foot they will want to move to take the next step.

Aside from the fact that, physically, it just won't work

(unless you hop), it does look rather curious, and it certainly doesn't feel like dancing.

So, how do you make certain your weight is where it should be?

"Lead with your head," says Don de Natale.

Actor-dancer de Natale co-starred with Geraldine Chaplin in the movie *Roseland* and was featured with Raquel Welch and James Coco in *Wild Party*. He is familiar to television viewers from coast to coast, talking, teaching, and dancing on talk shows, news programs, and telethons for muscular dystrophy, cerebral palsy, and Bob Hope's "Fight for Sight."

The de Natale secret is simple: If you're going to want to step left, just move your head toward the left, a bit ahead of the step you are about to take (a sort of look-where-you're-going technique).

"Your body and your weight will follow your head, and you'll find your weight is where you want it, on the correct foot, ready to sustain you for the next step."

It sounds too simple to be true, but it works. Or, as deNatale put it: "If you know where your head's at, you'll know where your weight is at."

★★

Here is why so many disco devotees can dance all night and feel great the next day. The exercise involved in disco dancing, experts say, causes these effects in the body:

*It increases the number of oxygen-carrying red blood cells.

*It improves the use of oxygen by body tissues.

*It aids digestion.

*It strengthens the heart and makes it work more efficiently.

*It builds stamina.

*It tones muscles.

*It helps relieve fatigue and tension.

*It helps balance your calorie intake and energy output.

★★

15

Last Dance

Billboard's Disco Forum IV 1978 Awards

The Disco Artist of the Year	Cerrone
Disco Artist of the Year (Female)	Donna Summer
Disco Artist of the Year (Male)	Cerrone
Disco Group of the Year (Male)	Village People
Most Promising New Disco Artist of the Year	Linda Clifford
Single of the Year—Heavy Disco/Light Radio	*A tie:* "Loving Is Really My Game" (Brainstorm) "Risky Changes" (Bionic Boogie)
Single of the Year—Heavy Disco/Heavy Radio	"Dance, Dance, Dance" (Chic)
Disco Single of the Year	"San Francisco/Hollywood"/"Fire Island" (Village People)
Disco Album of the Year	Bee Gees (and various), "Saturday Night Fever Soundtrack"
Disco Deejays' Favorite 12" Disco Disc	"Shame" (Evelyn King)

Disco Deejay of the Year
(National) .... Jim Burgess (Infinity, New York City)
Disco Composer of the Year .... Cerrone ("Cerrone III/Supernature" entire LP)
Best Producer of a
Disco Record .... Cerrone ("Cerrone's Paradise" & "Supernature—LPs by Cerrone——Africanism—LP by Kongas)
Disco Record Promotion
Person of the Year
(National In-House) .... Ray Caviano (TK Records)
Disco Record Promotion
Person of the Year
(National Independent) .... Tom Hayden (Tom Hayden & Assoc.)
Disco Music Arranger
of the Year .... Cerrone
Disco Instrumentalist
of the Year .... Cerrone
Disco Club Franchiser
of the Year .... Tom Jayson, 2001 Clubs

*Discothekin' Magazine Awards of 1978**

Best Disco, Nationwide: Studio 54
Best Regional Discos: Studio One in Los Angeles (which is now admitting women)
  Limelight, Florida
  Limelight, Montreal
Best Chic Disco: New York New York—for that touch of class
Best Women's Disco: Sahara, New York City
Best Latin, Black, and Rock Discos: Les Nuages, Pippin, Ashley's (New York)

*COURTESY OF 1978 DISCOTHEKIN' NEWS/DOCUMENT ARCHIVES

Most Improved Disco City: Los Angeles
Best Gay Disco: The Left (New York)
Best Over-All Design Firm: Design Circuit
Most Innovative Lighting Design: Jules Fisher, Studio 54
Best Sound System: Barry Lederer, 12 West

Michael O'Harro, owner of Tramps Disco in Washington, D. C., and a Billboard Forum Award winner, is generally known as the "Disco King." This is his list of the country's biggest disco cities:
- New York
- Los Angeles
- Washington, D. C.
- San Francisco
- Miami
- Dallas
- New Orleans
- Houston
- Chicago
- Wichita, Kansas
- Columbus and Cleveland, Ohio.

O'Harro names these as the country's top discos:
- Studio 54 and Regine's, New York
- Tramps (his own), Washington, D. C.
- Faces, Chicago
- Pips, Los Angeles
- Jubilation, Las Vegas
- California Club, Miami
- èlan, Dallas and Houston, Texas
- Casablanca, Tulsa, Oklahoma

About the Author

Kitty Hanson's byline appears in the New York *Daily News* above features, series, and exposés that have taken her and her readers from the streets of New York City's ghettos to the dance floors of its discotheques. Her work has earned for her and the *News* some fifteen major journalism awards for feature writing and crusading journalism, among them the George Polk Memorial Award, the Sigma Delta Chi Deadline Award, Society of Silurians awards, New York Reporters' Association Gold Typewriter and Byline awards, New York Newswomen's Club Front Page awards and New York Newspaper Guild Page One awards.

She is the author of *Rebels in the Streets* and *For Richer, for Poorer*, and with her husband, Hal Golden, who is senior vice-president of the United Way of Tri State, has co-authored two books, *Special Events* and *Working with the Working Press*. She is also the author of a number of documentary films.

A transplanted Hoosier who has flourished in the Manhattan asphalt, the author is a self-styled New York City "nut" and a gardening buff, and, with her husband, commutes between the city and an upstate 170-year-old hay barn the two of them have converted into a house. Her series on the disco phenomenon for the *News* turned her into a disco-"nut" as well, and when she is not dodging poison ivy or taxi cabs, she and her husband can be found disco dancing, which, they say, is a great way to keep fit, and more fun than jogging.

Other SIGNET Bestsellers You'll Want to Read

- [ ] **RAPTURE'S MISTRESS by Gimone Hall.** (#E8422—$2.25)*
- [ ] **MISTRESS OF OAKHURST—Book II by Walter Reed Johnson.** (#J8253—$1.95)
- [ ] **OAKHURST—Book I By Walter Reed Johnson.** (#J7874—$1.95)
- [ ] **I, JUDAS by Taylor Caldwell and Jess Stearn.** (#E8212—$2.50)
- [ ] **THE RAGING WINDS OF HEAVEN by June Shiplett.** (#J8213—$1.95)*
- [ ] **THE TODAY SHOW by Robert Metz.** (#E8214—$2.25)
- [ ] **HEAT by Arthur Herzog.** (#J8115—$1.95)*
- [ ] **THE SWARM by Arthur Herzog.** (#E8079—$2.25)
- [ ] **BEWARE MY HEART by Glenna Finley.** (#W8217—$1.50)*
- [ ] **I CAME TO THE HIGHLANDS by Velda Johnston.** (#J8218—$1.95)*
- [ ] **BLOCKBUSTER by Stephen Barlay.** (#E8111—$2.25)*
- [ ] **BALLET! by Tom Murphy.** (#E8112—$2.25)*
- [ ] **THE LADY SERENA by Jeanne Duval.** (#E8163—$2.25)*
- [ ] **SHADOW OF A BROKEN MAN by George Chesbro.** (#J8114—$1.95)*
- [ ] **LOVING STRANGERS by Jack Mayfield.** (#J8216—$1.95)*
- [ ] **BORN TO WIN by Muriel James and Dorothy Jongeward.** (#E8169—$2.50)*
- [ ] **THE HOURGLASS MAN by Carl Tiktin.** (#E8083—$1.75)
- [ ] **LOVERS IN A WINTER CIRCLE by Jonathan Kirsch.** (#E8119—$1.75)*
- [ ] **JULIE by Florence Stevenson.** (#J8121—$1.95)*

*Price slightly higher in Canada

Have You Read These Bestsellers from SIGNET?

☐ **ROGUE'S MISTRESS by Constance Gluyas.**
(#E8339—$2.25)

☐ **SAVAGE EDEN by Constance Gluyas.** (#E8338—$2.25)

☐ **WOMAN OF FURY by Constance Gluyas.** (#E8075—$2.25)*

☐ **BEYOND THE MALE MYTH by Anthony Pietropinto, M.D., and Jacqueline Simenauer.** (#E8076—$2.50)

☐ **CRAZY LOVE: An Autobiographical Account of Marriage and Madness by Phyllis Naylor.** (#J8077—$1.95)

☐ **THE SERIAL by Cyra McFadden.** (#J8080—$1.95)

☐ **HARMONY HALL by Jane Meredith.** (#E8082—$1.75)

☐ **DAMIEN—OMEN II by Joseph Howard.** (#J8164—$1.95)*

☐ **THE OMEN by David Seltzer.** (#J8180—$1.95)

☐ **THE RULING PASSION by Shaun Herron.** (#E8042—$2.25)

☐ **TWINS by Bari Wood and Jack Geasland.** (#E8015—$2.50)

☐ **CONSTANTINE CAY by Catherine Dillon.** (#J8307—$1.95)

☐ **WHITE FIRES BURNING by Catherine Dillon.**
(#J8281—$1.95)

☐ **THE WHITE KHAN by Catherine Dillon.** (#J8043—$1.95)*

☐ **FEAR OF FLYING by Erica Jong.** (#E7970—$2.25)

☐ **HOW TO SAVE YOUR OWN LIFE by Erica Jong.**
(#E7959—$2.50)*

☐ **KID ANDREW CODY AND JULIE SPARROW by Tony Curtis.** (#E8010—$2.25)*

☐ **THE MESSENGER by Mona Williams.** (#J8012—$1.95)

☐ **WINTER FIRE by Susannah Leigh.** (#E8011—$2.25)*

*Price slightly higher in Canada

NAL/ABRAMS' BOOKS
ON ART, CRAFTS AND SPORTS
in beautiful, large format, special concise editions—lavishly illustrated with many full-color plates.

- [ ] **THE ART OF WALT DISNEY: From Mickey Mouse to the Magic Kingdoms** by Christopher Finch. (#G9982—$7.95)
- [ ] **DISNEY'S AMERICA ON PARADE: A History of the U.S.A. in a Dazzling, Fun-Filled Pageant**, text by David Jacobs. (#G9974—$7.95)
- [ ] **FREDERIC REMINGTON** by Peter Hassrick. (#G9980—$6.95)
- [ ] **GRANDMA MOSES** by Otto Kallir. (#G9981—$6.95)
- [ ] **THE POSTER IN HISTORY** by Max Gallo. (#G9976—$7.95)
- [ ] **THE SCIENCE FICTION BOOK: An Illustrated History** by Franz Rottensteiner. (#G9978—$6.95)
- [ ] **NORMAN ROCKWELL: A Sixty Year Retrospective** by Thomas S. Buechner. (#G9969—$7.95)
- [ ] **THE PRO FOOTBALL EXPERIENCE** edited by David Boss, with an Introduction by Roger Kahn. (#G9984—$6.95)
- [ ] **THE DOLL** text by Carl Fox, photographs by H. Landshoff. (#G9987—$5.95)
- [ ] **DALI ... DALI ... DALI ...** edited and arranged by Max Gérard. (#G9983—$6.95)
- [ ] **THOMAS HART BENTON** by Matthew Baigell. (#G9979—$6.95)
- [ ] **THE WORLD OF M. C. ESCHER** by M. C. Escher and J. L. Locher. (#G9970—$7.95)

THE NEW AMERICAN LIBRARY, INC.,
P.O. Box 999, Bergenfield, New Jersey 07621

Please send me the SIGNET and ABRAMS BOOKS I have checked above. I am enclosing $_____ (please add 50¢ to this order to cover postage and handling). Send check or money order—no cash or C.O.D.'s. Prices and numbers are subject to change without notice.

Name _____

Address _____

City _____ State _____ Zip Code _____

Allow at least 4 weeks for delivery
This offer is subject to withdrawal without notice.